PRAISE FOR **DON'T SLEEP** WITH HIM *Yet*

"What *Lean In* did for women in business, *Don't Sleep with Him Yet* does for dating. Dr. Lee shows rare insight into the complex challenges today's women face regarding sex and relationships. Answering questions like why he disappears when things seem to be going fine, Lee explains how single women still mostly allow men to call all the shots. This fascinating book should be required reading for any woman seeking to empower herself in the dating world—and in everyday life. A game-changer."

—Jennifer Kaufman,
bestselling author of *Literacy
and Longing in LA; former
Los Angeles Times staff writer*

"Displaying unusual intelligence and wit, *Don't Sleep with Him Yet* stands alone as a wonderfully inspiring, badass *and* kick-ass '*Cosmopolitan* meets cool professor!' By far the best self-help book I've read in years."

—Katie S.,
copy editor.

"As a psychotherapist devoted to helping people improve relationship quality, I highly recommend Dr. Nancy Lee's book for anyone seeking a fulfilling romantic connection. Not only does Lee cut right to the chase of what's truly important, but I was also impressed by her hands-on examples of communications ranging from flirty texts to those dreaded 'What are we?' talks. Dr. Lee's advice won't just optimize your single life—rather, it will profoundly transform it."

—ernard Natelson, MBA, PsyD ABMP,
uthor of *Optimizing Your Single Life:
The Lost Art of Communication*

D0188178

"All my girlfriends tell me how 'lucky' I am to be engaged to my amazing fiancé. But it has nothing to do with luck. If it weren't for Dr. Lee, I'd still be kissing some narcissistic jerk-guy's butt — with nothing to show for it. Dr. Lee nails which guys to avoid at all costs. Read her book."

—Ashley S.,
luxury concierge services

"Smart, practical, fun to read, badass as promised. Drawing on her extensive research and experience in the field, Dr. Lee breaks it down for all of us who can't seem to get dating right and teaches us how to empower ourselves."

—Nina Sadowsky,
author of the romantic thrillers
Just Fall and *The Burial Society*

"If you want to stop the cycle of heartbreak and find and keep a long-term partner whose goal is to make you happy, read this book!"

—Sam Lewis,
author of *Don't Be an Idiot:
The Pyramid of Marital Success*

"Finally! A book that doesn't sugarcoat what's happening out there in the dating jungle. Most of all, Dr. Lee really wakes you up as to why we women keep settling for crumbs. (The patient with the porn-addicted boyfriend could have been me.) My only regret is that I didn't have *Don't Sleep with Him Yet* ten years ago — it would have spared me a lot of headaches and heartache."

—Jessica B.,
kindergarten teacher

"Dr. Nancy Lee's book has given me the knowledge and tools I needed to put myself back out there after a really nasty divorce. It's hard to believe I'm actually enjoying myself now, including an involvement with a loving, generous man. Thank you, Dr. Lee, for writing this badass book!"

—Olivia M.,
wealth management

"Completely in step with #MeToo, this book has not only taught me how to identify emotional blackmail, but also how to stop it. Read this book and then pass it along to your ex."

—Grace Kim,
graduate neuroscience studies

"Dr. Nancy Lee calls out some hard truths about casual hookups that nobody else seems willing to face. As a sexual assault survivor (committed by a 'friend' my freshman year of college) I can personally attest that her discussion about the 'New Rape Culture' is both brilliant and brave, spot on, compassionate. Most of all, it's immensely healing."

—Sarah A., law student

"Well-written and honest, this book relates to any woman from teens on up who has ever shoved aside her own true needs and desires just to 'fit in' or accommodate a guy."

—Lucy K.,
high school
guidance counselor

"*Don't Sleep with Him Yet* will turn your life around—whether you're single, straight or gay."

—Danielle L.,
advertising executive

"Sexy, edgy and often laugh-aloud-funny, *Don't Sleep with Him Yet* takes a scary dating scene and turns it on its head. This book has given me more stiletto power than any knockout shoes ever could. Loved the chapter on women's relation to beauty and the really great tips!"

—Raquel Richards, model

DON'T SLEEP WITH HIM *Yet*

DON'T SLEEP WITH HIM

Yet

A Badass Guide to Dating in 10 Empowering Steps

DR. NANCY LEE

MCP Books

MCP Books
2301 Lucien Way #415
Maitland, FL 32751
407.339.4217
www.millcitypress.net

Printed in the United States of America

ISBN-13: 9781545651766

Don't you think maybe they're the same thing?
Love and attention?

– Headmistress Sarah Joan, *Lady Bird*

CONTENTS

AUTHOR'S NOTE

The stories in this book are all true. However, to protect my patients' confidentiality I have changed names and identifying details where necessary.

This is for my girls all around the world
Who have come across a man that don't accept your worth

—Christina Aguilera

INTRODUCTION

I loved fairy tales as a kid; still do. Especially the ones where the perky heroine outsmarts evil detractors with the help of magical friends and eventually ends up with a charming (read: hot) prince. We typically don't know much about the hero-prince other than that he's a great kisser. In fact, in fairy tales, hero and heroine seem to go straight from that first wake-up kiss to happily ever after, no dating involved.

Not so in the real world. Even the remote possibility of a happy ending generally involves some heavy-duty dating, not to mention kissing all those frogs. And despite it all, you still find yourself not in the enchanted castle you deserve with your own prince of a guy by your side, but in bed — with a toad. Or, even worse, with a guy you thought was a prince; that is, until you never hear from him again.

Dating these days has increasingly become less magically exciting and more a heart-wrenching, uncharted minefield punctuated by way too many WTF moments. If you find your-self checking your phone far too often for any kind of word (or hope) from some guy you're seeing who seems to have mostly checked out, then you're not alone. Staggering numbers of women currently lament that their love lives, if they even have them, are unsatisfactory. Women describe that paradoxically, despite feeling free to do as they please, they nevertheless act as slaves to pressures beyond their control. Particularly troubling is an unspoken social pressure to sleep with someone you're dating not out of authentic desire, but out of misguided obliga-tion. Yes, it really is possible to be too "polite," especially if your people-pleasing tendencies compel you to consent to, or perhaps more accurately *cave to* sex you don't actually want. There is too much at stake—intimacy, romance, love, friendships, and, yes, really good sex—to let that happen. Not to mention your sanity. Listen up, ladies: "free" is not the same as *empowered.*

For instance, there's a big difference between embracing and enjoying your sexuality, and treating it as though it were an everyday expendable. Conversely, you'll learn why sex makes a poor bartering chip. And you may be shocked to discover that your prince charming is already planning his exit strategy even while agreeing to be exclusive when you sleep together.

This book in no way whatsoever purports to have all the answers. But it is at once a true-story-filled page-turner, as well as a proven go-to for practically any dating scenario imaginable. Perhaps you can relate to the following sampling of questions I'm frequently asked:

- Why aren't any of the guys I meet interested in serious relationships?
- Am I crazy to pursue this guy despite all the red flags?
- Why hasn't he called even though we totally hit it off on that first date?
- How do I deal with the pressure to sleep with someone before I'm ready?
- If I wasn't into it, why hadn't I told him to stop?
- Why don't I seem to have luck with online dating? And how else can I meet new guys?
- Should I stay with someone I'm not completely happy with to avoid being alone?

Don't Sleep with Him Yet shows how to reclaim your own power so that dating and sex bring many more "Hell, yes!" times for you rather than being, well, merely hellacious. Likewise, your real-life ever after needn't be a purgatory of pain and regret. Simply put, let's bring back the magic.

How This Book Got Started

I hadn't set out to become an expert on dating. Originally I started out doing cognitive-behavioral therapy for depression and eating disorders. But a few years ago I noticed something curious in my thirty-year psychology practice. Nearly every week I had at least one new patient who happened to be attractive *and* personable, ranging in age from early twenties on up. Remarkably, these female patients were all presenting for therapy after having been dumped by the guys they were dating. The men initially came on very strong to these beautiful, dynamic women, and the nonstop texting and back-to-back dates also continued for a while in the beginning. One of the guys had even begun discussing marriage and children with my patient. (Side note: men will say just about anything to sleep with you.) Also, these women had much more going for them than just their looks. The group included: college students and recent graduates, law students, teachers, models, working actresses, production assistants, a medical intern, a neonatal nurse, an investment banker, an NBA cheerleader, a life coach, a dentist, an advertising executive, an entrepreneurial camgirl, a high-end bottle-service girl, a VIP concierge, and an entertainment agent, among others. The women were supersmart, except when it came to men. Bottom line: regardless of their looks and talents, the women were all rather unceremoniously dropped by the men whom they'd been dating — and sleeping with.

My patients had become romantically and emotionally attached to these outwardly "great" guys whose smarts and personalities were all over the map. Likewise, their financial statuses ranged from some serious student debt to loaded. However, intentional or not, these men were primarily posers. Meaning they were being nice and appearing emotionally available and commitment-ready, but there was no substance there. It wasn't that the guys weren't sincere at the time, it's just that they couldn't or wouldn't follow through. These dudes would say and do all the right things in order to have a relationship that included great sex for a few weeks or months, like a series of hookups with the same woman. Not long afterward, however, would come the inevitable text (yes, always the text), saying the guy just "wasn't ready for a relationship" after all or "had too much going on." It happens so often there's even a new slang name for these mostly millennial men who go for a woman's heart and soul in addition to her panties: "softboys." Some of my patients didn't even receive the courtesy of a breakup text. Instead their partners just stopped calling, texting, or communicating altogether; in other words, they simply disappeared. Once again, the frequency of this behavior has resulted in the now-common slang term: "to ghost."

In my book, however, all these dudes are pathetic cowards who don't want to face the recipient of their guilt-ridden, dubious behavior. Because how do you tell a woman whom you've been sleeping with that the initial excitement is over and you've become bored with her or, worse yet, that you were never really all that into her in the first place? And even when the guy is truly into his partner, he takes her for granted, perhaps lured by a seemingly global glut of girls. So he gambles away something solid and great with a mouse click or swipe of his thumb. As their therapist/dating advisor, and with the wisdom that only years of life experience brings, I knew intuitively that the heartache these wonderful women were experiencing had much to do with their uninformed (okay, clueless), conformity-driven, overly acquiescent behavior. But as a clinical psychologist who views human behavior from a scientific vantage point, I needed proof. Hence, Step 9, "Don't Sleep with Him Yet," and the seed for this book was born.

During the course of my research on sexual behavior, I discovered fascinating studies, surveys, facts, and experiments regarding all realms of dating, mating, and attraction. I found myself discussing these findings with countless women and men nearly daily in my private practice. And guess what? The women, especially, began to assert what they needed and wanted (or didn't want) from dating partners, instead of just blindly following the guy's lead. They also began to stand up to both new and longstanding partners who didn't treat them well.

Call it a personally tailored Time's Up. What's more, unattached patients (happily) reported that they were not only meeting and attracting far more men, but they also were realizing deeper connections and genuine commitment, which had previously eluded them.

It's not that I possess any secret formula for dating (although sometimes I wish I did). But I do have "an ear" on both sides of the dating equation: women *and* men. Especially noteworthy is that as a psychologist, I hear men's innermost thoughts and feelings — and desires. Daily. So in addition to being entrusted with the dating and relationship challenges women constantly face, I've got insider knowledge as to how men's minds work, including what's uniquely problematic for them as well.

Which is partly why I can prove that women and men occupy two entirely different emotional demographics. Still, you'll be surprised to learn that large percentages of single guys have the exact same goals as you. That is, they want to find a woman they're attracted to romantically who may potentially become a trusted, adored life partner. *Don't Sleep with Him Yet* reveals how to attract these men instead of the ones who keep letting you down. You and the (good) men whom you choose to date both want to win the same game: I show you how to become cherished teammates rather than misunderstood opponents.

Notably, the 10 Steps constitute a logical, easy-to-follow format geared toward finding a partner and establishing a committed relationship; consider it a dating GPS. And, yes, although this book is technically about dating, I also show you how to artfully apply its core message of female empowerment to related areas of your life, from building self-confidence to eliminating knee-jerk people-pleasing. Strength. Knowledge. Informed choices. That's badass and what this book is all about.

Let's Get Physical: Nothing's Off-Limits

Then there's the proverbial elephant in the room. Namely, something many other psychologists miss — or may feel hesitant to talk about. It's that as women, we have wondrous, if all too often underappreciated, "hardware" from the neck down that warrants just as much discussion as our minds. Not only is important emotional territory covered, but so is physical attraction—both key to a successful dating relationship. Assuming it's mutual, women want to be desired. At *any* age. Unlike other dating books written by psychologists, your appearance and sexual satisfaction are not considered off-limits. Whether it's solid academic reasoning or girlfriend-to-girlfriend hot tips, I give them both to you. Straight up.

Also, my claims are supported with reams of credible research from the fields of psychology, psychobiology, neuroscience, evolutionary psychology, computational sociology, and even business. *Don't Sleep with Him Yet* references top science because you deserve no less. Intriguing, cutting-edge facts will affect your life in a remarkably powerful way that's realistically in sync with today's sexual norms, partly by lending clarity when you may be going through an especially confusing time— or blurry looking glass. Which is also why I delve deeply into emotional blackmail at the core of coercive sex. In fact, I was already exploring the murky, "gray" zone of sexual consent as a professional participant on college panels promoting sexual assault prevention long before the #MeToo movement hit. Too many young women today find out eye-opening truths the hard way; you don't have to.

Refreshingly, I also don't assume that all of you are looking for husbands; in today's world of highly accomplished, independent women, many opt out of marriage. So I make it a point to address confirmed singletons' needs and issues just as thoroughly as I do those of you who are seeking marriage. You may have more in common than you think.

Ultimately, I wrote this book simply because I want you, dear reader, to experience the joy of romance, passion, great sex, and, yes, love. I'll show you exactly how to get to that place of genuine physical and emotional intimacy and connectedness with men—and more. Dating shouldn't be warfare: let's get you out of the trenches.

♫ **Side note:** When it comes to love—not to mention longing— music triggers powerful feelings variously layered in memory or entirely new. (A select bunch of "says-it-best" song lyrics sprinkled throughout the book are referenced by title at the end of each Step, as well as in Appendix 1: The Playlist.) So whether or not you're currently in the market for a keeper-boyfriend or are strictly in "girls just wanna have fun" mode, it's time to join me on a smart, sexy tour through *Don't Sleep with Him Yet* that is going to rock your world.

Introduction Playlist ♫
Can't Hold Us Down/Christina Aguilera
Girls Just Wanna Have Fun/Cyndi Lauper

INTRODUCING THE 10 STEPS

Part I: Getting Psyched for Dating

Step 1—You Go Girl: Making It Happen explains how to let go of self-doubt and begin to trust in yourself and your decisions. Regardless of your choices, you'll learn how to communicate what you want to a new man in your life without scaring him away and why a woman's authenticity draws relationships where she is desired and valued. Step 1 additionally showcases how every generation of women from boomers on has influenced sexual attitudes and behaviors. You'll discover why millennials in particular really can have it all.

Step 2—Attitude Twerking: Confidence, Optimism, Mindfulness, and Enthusiasm Are Sexy shows how Confidence, Optimism, Mindfulness, and Enthusiasm (COME) attract romance and bring about successful outcomes—in any realm. These four attributes at the core of positive psychology work wonders in and outside the bedroom: they have the potential to boost both your overall personal happiness and professional pursuits, too. As for the opposite effect, or happiness hijackers, Step 2 additionally takes a look at social media, revealing its dark side, including the way it can chip away at self-esteem.

Step 3—Hard Truths: All About Men (and Which to Avoid) provides unique, spot-on insight into men based on their chronological age, including the *real* truth about that fortysomething guy's midlife "crisis." Can't figure out dudes? Then refer to the chart of Men's Emotional Maturation to find out exactly what makes them tick. Perhaps most important of all is the brutal exposé of seriously flawed men such as serial philanderers, narcissists, and emotional manipulators, to name just a few. (Beware of heartbreak ahead!) Step 3 also recounts alarming personal experiences of women who were involved with the most toxic of these guys.

Part II: Igniting a Romantic Connection

Step 4—Finding Him: Step Out of Your Comfort Zone indicates where to find single men and demonstrates the most effective ways to meet the ones you actually want to date. You'll be inspired by very specific suggestions as well as encouraging stories of patients who came to me in a dating rut before meeting their current boyfriends. Crucially, Step 4 also describes the most common way couples meet (online ranks second most common) and explores how to apply that to your present life circumstances. The straight-up lowdown on pricey matchmaking services will also help you decide if that's an option for you.

Step 5—Hooking Up: More Than Just Friends is invaluable if you wish you were more than just friends with him. This step reveals when and how a friendship can become a romance; furthermore, there is actually a scientific basis for why you and that guy friend may fall in love. At the opposite end of the romantic spectrum, Step 5 shows which sexual hookups and (bad) dates run rife with resentment for women; emotional blackmail at the core of coercive sex is finally called out. Plus, you'll glean rare insight into what psychologically drives the "new" rape culture on college campuses.

Step 6—Do Online Smart: Myths and Musts unravels and clarifies vital data showing which profile features attract the best matches on Internet dating sites and how to increase your odds of meeting someone right for you. Not sure how much to reveal? Let me help you out! The pros and cons of five popular dating apps are also discussed, including which "type" of man uses each one. Step 6 additionally explains the psychologically seductive allure of online relationships and why women in particular are so easily drawn in.

Step 7 — Light His Fire: Why He Can't Stop Thinking About You breaks down exactly how a man becomes captivated by you, including the neuropsychology of sexual attraction and romantic love. Like casting a (real) love spell, Step 7 details surefire ways to get noticed – from subtle signals to killer eye contact. The Step additionally explains how you and a potential partner truly become close and what makes that closeness so incredibly thrilling. Unless, of course, he's married, which Step 7 covers as well. The difference between flirting and harassment is also clearly spelled out (hint: pleasing or *please don't*) — and there's nothing "gray" about this one at all.

Step 8 — Letting Go: When and How to Move On — or Move In offers advice for when to contact a guy after an early date, and also illuminates the ten most common reasons why he doesn't call. Can't resist texting him just once more? Then follow Step 8's texting sample dos and don'ts. You'll also learn to read the sometimes subtle signs of a long-term boyfriend who is not necessarily leading you on – so much as leading you nowhere. What's more, Step 8 scientifically shows why rejection hurts so much and how to handle the pain, and most importantly, move on. As for happier times, Step 8 helps you decide whether you should move in with him or not.

Part III: Making It Last: Commitment, Passion, and Sex

Step 9 — The New Choice: Don't Sleep with Him Yet presents groundbreaking research that reveals why sex is actually more gratifying for both men and women after a waiting period with a new partner. Step 9 also reports what men say about today's fast-paced sexual marketplace, including why it is often crazy-making for them as well. Consider Step 9 as a very, very loud wake-up call. This Step will show you how to tell when the time is right (if ever) to sleep with a guy regardless of what you want out of the relationship. In a related vein, you'll learn how to handle pressure to have sex before you're ready with someone you like and wish to keep dating.

Step 10 — Bring It: Best. Sex. Ever. (*Your* Choice) introduces a bold, sensual new way to enjoy sex that focuses on your own pleasure as well as on his; things finally heat up for *both* of you. This is especially important considering the evidence that women aren't actually enjoying sex much these days. The seriously seductive, sensually focused material — including a one-page erotic exercise you can use with your partner — will turn you on just reading it. What's more, you'll learn clinically proven ways to keep your sex life fresh and exciting with a long-standing partner.

Just for Fun: Empowering Extras

Hot Stuff: From Plain to Pretty, and Pretty to Drop-Dead Gorgeous explores women's relationship to beauty from intriguing new psychosocial perspectives, including how cosmetics make us happy and an economist's provocative theory that better looking people attract higher earning spouses. Empowering Extras additionally spill the best (but remarkably simple) beauty tips from top Hollywood experts. Among other Hot Stuff highlights: how to prevent the common, creeping weight gain that happens after age twenty-five; what surprising physical feature men actually notice immediately; and whether you should pursue that plastic surgery procedure you've been considering — or not.

Part 1:

GETTING PSYCHED FOR DATING

Everybody stands as she goes by
'Cause they can see the flame that's in her eyes
Watch her when she's lighting up the night . . . This girl is on fire

—Alicia Keys

Step 1

You Go Girl: Making It Happen

*D*ating can be great. Or not. Then again, if it's never fun for you something is off. That doesn't mean that you won't experience some just plain awful "What the heck am I doing here?" moments or downright defeating "I'd rather be home with my dog than dealing with this jerk" dates. And let's not forget the out-of-left-field heartache that long-term lovers often toss our way. Nevertheless, the times that dating builds you up should far outnumber the times it beats you down.

Memo to all women who are masters of self-blame: very few of us manage to escape the occasional romantic misread or sucker punch of a rejection. So stop being so hard on yourself! As an astute *LA Times* human-interest journalist recently mused, "We are better than our worst mistakes." That doesn't mean you need to let your guard down or not be accountable for your decisions. It just means that as we go about our lives, we do the best with the information and experience we have on hand; circumstances and perspective that lead to regret only appear later. (For example, how could you have known that the sweet guy you've been dating for a year would end up cheating on you — with another guy?) In fact, all those prior trip-ups will actually enhance your joy when things eventually do come together, whether in regard to relationships or any other important goals.

Along these lines, keep in mind that what feels right when you're twenty-two may be very different from what you want when you're thirty-seven. Or forty-seven. No matter your age, however, it is self-respect, not self-recrimination that will see you through some potentially tough experiences without becoming waylaid by frustration or saddled with regrets. In other words: stop beating yourself up and give yourself the slack that allows you to move forward with trust in yourself and others.

As for how to get to that sweet spot where self-confidence and self-respect meet your own longing and lust, you've got to start somewhere. This first Step introduces common dating prototypes women are faced with today. Additionally, although most women believe they are making independent decisions regarding relationships, you may recognize yourself in the discussion below of how societal forces have influenced different generations of women (baby boomers, Gen Xers, and millennials) to choose anything from casual sex with multiple partners on through monogamous, marriage-in-mind sex. Most important of all, if your own approach to dating and sex is wearing you down or not getting you what you want, you'll find out why.

If You Want a Ring

In fact, your approach to dating, or getting to know someone romantically, comes down to intention. For example, do you seek an "OMG he's amazing," bonded-for-life soul mate (okay, even if he's just short of amazing)? Or are you simply dying for that heart-cute Facebook "in-a relationship" status? If so, down the line will you settle for no less than an engagement ring? If you answered yes to any of these questions, then dating for you is a means to an end, and it is therefore important to clarify your goals. Cognitive-behavioral psychology has credibly demonstrated that if a person has well-defined, clear goals, she is far more likely to reach them than if her goals are vague or amorphous.

In fact, a quest to find some form of emotional intimacy or love, or both, with a romantic partner is common across cultures. Along with satisfying sex, this could be considered a birthright. (Not to mention the benefits of a duel income or the ease and enjoyment of having a ready partner with whom to paint the town—or travel the world.) However, even though a vast majority of adult American women of all ages still say that they ultimately desire a monogamous relationship with a boyfriend or husband, these same women are afraid to acknowledge their own needs or goals, particularly to new men in their lives, for fear of being viewed as too serious or "just about marriage." But the reality is that research shows the reverse to be true; women who are candid with men about what they want attract men with similar goals and values.

Know that there are plenty of great guys out there who are looking for a keeper-girlfriend. In fact, nationwide Pew polls report that 76 percent of American adults are either married or wish to be. (Census studies show that 51 percent of Americans aged eighteen and up are actually married.) That doesn't mean you need to discuss babies and bridal registries on your first date; there is a difference between being desperately fanatical versus merely honest with a man about what you want in life. So if you pretend to be a casual dater while hiding your true needs and desires, then don't be surprised or hurt when your dates respond in kind—by casually moving on from you to someone else. At the same time, women who search for a long-term mate as persistently as they'd pursue a professional goal are those who do realize, if not necessarily the full-on happily-ever-after, at least some semblance of it.

Endgame Optional

If you aren't as end-goal-oriented as some of your bridal-magazine-toting sorority sisters, here's an alternate set of questions: Are you a woman who is having fun and wants to keep lots of guy-options open? Might you be a very inexperienced dater who is just beginning to learn about herself in relation to the opposite sex? Perhaps including sexual experimentation? Conversely, are you a woman who is regaining her footing in the dating world after a lapse of several years, perhaps by virtue of divorce or widowhood?

Interestingly, the number of women who fall into any one of these diverse categories is on the rise. A recently coined term, "coconspirators," refers to dating partners who enjoy each other's company and may share intimacies, but don't necessarily seek long-term involvement. (Although many newly divorced or widowed women I know actually *are* looking for committed partners.) Nevertheless, depending on your situation, it can be tremendously liberating as one patient put it, "to not be all about the endgame." Endgame or not, you'll still be confronted with many of the same issues as your soul-mate-seeking sisters; not the least of which is deciding which guys you actually want to spend time with and how much of yourself to give to the relationship.

Respect Yourself

When it comes to "outside" pressures, even though there'll always be that one annoying relative who pesters you about whether you're seeing anyone "special," not everyone will be on your case, as would have been the situation years ago. It's just not PC anymore. For good reason. Today's enlightened women are much freer to make their own personal choices without societal judgment. There's no longer the *universal* expectation that a woman will eventually get married, nor is there a social stigma if she doesn't. And this doesn't just apply to women with high-powered careers; the loosening of traditional expectations applies to women across varied socioeconomic strata. True — societal convention coupled with religious tenets have ensured that marriage as an institution is here to stay. Yet cultural practices have evolved to the point that almost anything goes insofar as what contemporary women want — or don't want — and how they conduct their lives. So instead of dodging cousin Fred and his intrusive questions at the next family reunion, *own* your response (and current singlehood) that of course there is someone special in your life — yourself.

It is wonderful that women truly are as empowered as men in choosing their interpersonal lifestyles for perhaps the first time.

The problem is that this newfound freedom has also emboldened many women to act far more cavalier about dating and relationships than they actually are. Specifically, women who secretly entertain hopes of commitment often pose as indifferent to the whole dating experience in general, disavowing their personal goals in the process. So you sleep with a guy you're hoping for a relationship with, he starts pulling away — and you pretend you don't care.

Consistent with feigned indifference, women who attempt to convince themselves that almost any neglectful or otherwise hurtful behavior a dating partner engages in is acceptable tend to be treated uniformly poorly by a wide range of men. Men really do prefer, and respect, women who challenge them over doormat dates whom they can easily step on — and later step over as they walk out the door. For example, I've heard over and over from men that even though they may be variously disappointed, whiny, and unhappy when a woman they're dating won't sleep with them right away, they nevertheless respect that woman's choice — and the way she stood up for herself. Consider: bad*ass* and *ass*ertiveness have crucial common ground.

While there are some demands that women can't make outright of men (e.g., love), they can demand respect. Even the irreverent Howard Stern, who would normally be the last person on earth pegged with defending women's rights, admonished years ago that "No woman should put up with a guy who acts like I do on the radio." But, regrettably, many women do.

Until now, that is.

Hopefully the "trickle-down" effect of both #MeToo and Time's Up movements will finally stop women from self-doubting themselves into silence even in consensual relationships, whether with a new love interest or a longtime love. In both cases the message is: be true to yourself. It is critical to realize that with romance in play, we women wish to be desired, valued, and, depending on the nature of the relationship, loved and treasured by the men we let into our lives. Hence, truly empowered women go after what they want: they follow their own interpersonal roadmaps, traversing blurred lines between lust and love, but all the while demanding respect. Dignity, self-respect, and choice set the precedent for all-new female-centric dating.

I Am Woman (Hear Me Roar)

Let's finally make this a *woman's* world, girlfriend.

None of us lives in a vacuum. Whether we realize it or not, forces outside ourselves, particularly intergenerational forces, continually shape our behaviors and actions. Then there's the flip side that you can make a big difference to others down the line, too. Because regardless of how young or old you are, know that you're part of a precious sisterhood whose voices continue to echo through an endless tunnel of time. But first those voices have to be heard.

Baby Boomers: Feminist Revolutionaries with Romantic Misgivings

Baby boomer women (born between 1946 and 1964) came of age in the era of Betty Friedan's *Feminine Mystique*, Gloria Steinem's feminist activism, the Equal Rights Amendment, and NOW (National Organization for Women). These women were constantly striving for equality with men in the workplace and political arenas. Understandably, they also extended this fight for equality into the bedroom, attempting to prove that women can behave sexually just like men.

However, while it is absolutely imperative for women to gain equal job opportunities and make as much as their male counterparts, psychobiological constraints do not confer equal-opportunity sleeping around as readily beneficial to women—a lesson that idealistic female boomers learned much later by experience. (Step 9 will clearly explain how such constraints, especially those rooted in emotional brain structure and hormones, as well as in evolutionary and cultural forces, drive men's and women's fundamentally different approaches to sex and attachment.) Most women would agree that being rightfully afforded the same sexual choices and freedom as men should not mean we have to forego meaningful emotional intimacy and heightened passion. That said, what boomer women gained in terms of sexual equality was often lost in a labyrinth of loveless liaisons bereft of romance. In fact, a recurring lament in therapy, particularly among never-married Woodstock-era boomer women, is that they regret *consistently* having treated their sexuality as casually as they used to. This running therapeutic theme among some of my patients also corroborates an unintended consequence of the sexual revolution of the '60s, which was supposed to free women of sexual oppression and constraints. But that success came at a cost: the socially sanctioned dismissal of women's sexual-emotional needs by men. Only much later would both sexes concede that sexual freedom and emotional connection are not mutually exclusive.

Generation X Women: Conventional Cynics

In contrast to their idealistic, free-spirited boomer counterparts, Generation X females (born between 1965 and 1981) are actually highly conventional. This is contrary to popular myth, which views Gen X women as shunning marriage and family. As evidence, Stuart Michaels, PhD, one of the principal investigators for the landmark nineties-era National Health and Social Life Survey, concluded, "Those coming of age after AIDS actually behave more conservatively than their predecessors."

The study went on to note that Generation Xers of both sexes value fidelity and have one partner at a time. However, having witnessed the high divorce rate of their boomer predecessors, Gen X females nonetheless developed highly cynical attitudes toward marriage. That cynicism, as well as delaying marriage and family in the pursuit of career, contributed to Generation Xers' postponement of marriage until the age of thirty. This is significantly older than earlier generations, whose age of first marriage is consistently reported in the twenties. Therefore, although the study found that Gen X women ultimately seek monogamy, these women also were found to have many more sexual partners before and between long-term relationships (to wit: *Sex and the City*'s archetypal Gen X female Carrie Bradshaw). Thus, as the study emphasized, an epidemic of STDs was born.

Particularly disconcerting is chlamydia, an often symptom-free disease infecting both men and women that is transmitted by vaginal, oral, and anal sex. Left untreated, chlamydia can cause permanent damage to women's reproductive organs. In fact, according to officials, ever since 1992 it has ranked first among undiagnosed STDs that cause twenty thousand women in the United States to become infertile each year.

And the news just gets worse.

As reported in a 2015 *Los Angeles Times* Health Watch, "The volume of chlamydia cases last year was particularly staggering. Nationwide there were about 1.4 million cases, which is the highest number of any condition ever reported to the Centers for Disease Control (CDC)." Hitting home, more Californians were diagnosed with chlamydia in 2017 than ever before, according to state public health officials. Notably, one significant risk factor for chlamydia is the number of sexual partners within the past year. That fact alone may give women pause: there really is no free ride, so to speak.

The good news is that chlamydia is preventable with use of a condom—assuming it doesn't break. Which is yet another reason to cover your ass and insist that your partner be tested for STDs before sleeping with him.

Millennials: Feminism at Its Best

Millennial women (born between 1982 and 2003) have inherited the best of preceding generations. They've maintained the idealism of their boomer mothers, who forged the path for sexual freedom and workplace gender equality. Similarly, millennial women were largely raised as the children of loving, richly involved parents, who instilled a confident "shoot for the stars" approach to life. At the same time, young women today have also held on to the valuable pragmatism of their Gen X sisters, minus the cynicism. As Morley Winograd and Michael Hais note in their illuminating book, *Millennial Momentum,* approximately 58 percent of college students are women, and once in college, women seem to accomplish as much, if not more than, men. Quoting Department of Education statistics, Winograd and Hais note that women are more likely to get bachelor's degrees and better college grades than men. They also earn a higher (by approximately 10 to 20 percent) proportion of advanced degrees, including masters and doctorates. Winograd and Hais conclude: "These achievements have produced a generation of self-confident women who, unlike many of their boomer mothers and grandmothers, do not see themselves in conflict or competition with men." (Note that competition is not the same as putting up with sexist injustices like paying women less than men for the same job, which are being called out by who else but millennials such as accomplished actress Jennifer Lawrence.) Similarly, on her "Next Great Generation" website, Jen Kalaidis, a millennial herself, defines a new "millennial feminism": "Today's women were raised to believe we were equal to men, but we didn't have to try to be them to prove it."

What a relief.

This no-nonsense, egalitarian attitude has phenomenal implications for all women caught up in today's dating kaleidoscope. Essentially, there no longer exists a sociocultural zeitgeist for women to operate like men when it comes to sex, as in men will sleep with nearly anyone. As Kalaidis's remarks suggest, women as a group no longer have anything to prove. Ironically, female millennials' peer-influenced "permission" to forego casual sex today appears just as hard going as their predecessors' sexual freedom was hard-earned. Consider: in the '70s through the early '80s, with abstinence by then considered uncool, college women were often embarrassed to tell their girlfriends that they weren't having sex. Case in point: decades later one of my two senior-year apartment roommates confided that they'd actually searched through my drawers for (non-existent) pills or a diaphragm because they couldn't figure out what birth control I was using. Some of the men were not much better. One especially arrogant senior frat guy's parting shot to me (as a freshman) was his "warning" that nobody would ever want to date me, simply because I wouldn't get naked and make out with him the first—and only—time we went out.

The independent, confident millennial woman no longer has to put up with any of that BS. How and when sex fits into her life is entirely up to her. The point is that a woman's decisions and choices are hers alone—not a product of blind conformity, undue pressure, or the need to compete or prove equal sexual footing with men. Speaking of competition, even digital downloads have wreaked havoc with women's psyches unnecessarily over the past few decades. Specifically, please don't think that you have to compete with internet porn, despite its ubiquity. Most men eventually realize that a beefed-up, waxed-down cyber version of a woman is no match for a real woman, pubic hair and all.

The power of *choice* is both liberating and key: a millennial woman can say no just as confidently as she can say yes. Furthermore, a millennial's "no," or any other woman's for that matter, needn't come with an apology when it involves access to our precious bodies. And that fact truly heralds the exciting new spirit of today's "bedroom feminism," or perhaps more aptly, female empowerment. Empowerment is all about going for what *you* truly want and making it happen. It isn't that other generations of women couldn't have it all; they just thought they couldn't. Not so for motivated she-millenials. When it comes to love, sex, and careers—millennial girl, the world is yours for the taking. And, yes, little sister, you really are on fire.

Step 1 Playlist ♫
Girl on Fire/Alicia Keys
Respect Yourself/Melissa Etheridge
I Am Woman (Hear Me Roar)/Helen Reddy
♫ **Side note:** I've showcased a female iconic singer/songwriter from each generation (boomer, Gen X, and millennial) based on their longstanding influence on sexual attitudes and behaviors. Who would you choose? (See Appendix 2)

Listen as your day unfolds, challenge what the future holds, try and keep your head up to the sky
You gotta be bad, you gotta be bold, you gotta be wiser

—Des'ree

Step 2

Attitude Twerking: Confidence, Optimism, Mindfulness, and Enthusiasm Are Sexy

*A*li is a statuesque twenty-eight-year-old blonde who turns heads wherever she goes. She also happens to be a record-setting long-distance runner. However, Ali was beyond despondent when she first started seeing me; her live-in boyfriend had dumped her, and somehow she believed the breakup was all her fault. Ditto for her other past long-term relationship. It soon became clear that Ali was gravitating toward emotionally abusive men who devalued her. How could someone this beautiful and talented find herself so miserable in her romantic life? The answer soon became clear: low self-confidence. Essentially, she was limiting herself through self-doubt and fear.

Or, as I told Ali, it's all in your attitude.

To note, I live and work in the entertainment capital of America, and I interact both professionally and socially with some of the most gorgeous women on this planet. My patients include knockout playmates as well as celebrities who top "most beautiful" lists. Not to mention the occasional international beauty pageant winner. And living just a whisper away from Hollywood, I actually found myself sipping Chardonnay at a pool party recently while wondering why most of the (other) women looked like swimsuit models — until the host happily pointed out that they actually were! (Gulp) Nevertheless, one day I was caught off guard by an exceptionally sexy woman — and she wasn't a twenty-three-year-old bombshell/aspiring starlet. Rather, this mesmerizing goddess speaking at a 2006 Los Angeles book fair was then-sixty-four-year-old Erica Jong, author of the groundbreaking 1973 sexual novel *Fear of Flying*. Simply put, she was magnificent. Her sexy magnetism was expressed in her open, sensual, positive attitude toward life. And the one word following "For Dr. Nancy" on her book inscription to me sums it all up, "Fearlessly." Or in other words: badass.

Whether she's twenty-one or eighty-one, today's badass woman has a winning, courageous attitude marked by: Confidence, Optimism, Mindfulness, and Enthusiasm (denoted by the acronym COME, as in COME to a new attitude). She doesn't shrink from life but rather meets its challenges head on with inner strength and spirited resolve, that is, *fearlessly.*

"You Got This": Lucky 7 Confidence Boosters

- Integrate positive affirmations ("I am smart, funny, kind, etc.")
- Overrate to motivate
- Keep a permanent list in your head of times you aced it
- Practice, practice, practice! (Overlearning builds confidence)
- Don't overthink: "Just Do It"
- Take risks (associated with self-fulfilling prophecy/ good outcomes)
- Do not compare and despair (social media)

Confidence

The word confidence is derived from the Latin *confidere*, meaning to trust, or have faith in. Self-confidence is not some sort of personality gift bestowed by the gods above, but rather a consistent trust or belief in one's self and one's abilities. And really, when you think about it, if you can't trust yourself, why should anyone else?

If you feel lacking in the self-assurance arena, practice daily affirmations, actually telling yourself that: *I am smart, sexy, generous, kind,* etc., and it won't be long before you begin to automatically integrate and express these aspects of your personality. Psychologists refer to this as "positive illusions" or instinctively overrating our abilities to believe we're a bit better/funnier/ more capable than we are; this works to rev up confidence and motivate us in challenging situations. For example, you may choose to go to a party or **other social** event alone that you'd otherwise avoid (and miss out on **meeting** potential dating partners). There are infinite numbers of possible affirmations. Check out some of my favorites:

1. I'm a good problem solver.
2. I don't put up with crap.
3. I give things my all.
4. I don't sweat the small stuff.
5. "I woke up like this (flawless)." –Beyoncé

Another practical confidence booster is to keep a running list in your head of times where you felt especially good about yourself; for example, you threw a great party — or a winning clutch shot — or you aced an exam or got promoted at work, or you helped someone in need. Or the list could simply include snapshots in time that you remember as particularly special; for instance, winding down a perfect day at the beach watching a spectacular sunset. Then, whenever you need an extra shot of confidence — perhaps before an anxiously anticipated first date — summon up that list and let your mind travel back to those uplifting moments in time. It really works: you'll find yourself in a much better place mentally to face whatever lies ahead.

Also, don't underestimate the power of practice. The late legendary psychologist Albert Ellis, PhD, largely regarded as the second most influential psychotherapist in history, told the *New York Times* that at the painfully shy age of nineteen he forced himself to approach two hundred women who sat down alone at a park bench over a period of a month at the Bronx Botanical Garden. Out of this group, he reportedly got one date (who apparently never showed up). But Ellis himself boasted that all that changed with the "second one hundred" resulting in several actual dates. The widely popular lecturer also forced himself early on to speak over and over to groups in order to become confident at public speaking, which he once viewed as "a fate worse than public masturbation." Likewise, consider beauty pageant winner and three-time Oscar nominee Michelle Pfeiffer; by her own admission, only with extended practice did she overcome a "paralyzing" fear of small talk. In other words, overlearning a skill builds confidence. Even world-class gymnasts who awe the world with flawless, body-bending feats spend hours upon hours perfecting their moves — and recharging their confidence — every day. To exemplify, what did the "Fab 5" 2016 USA Olympic Gymnastics team champions report pumped them up most to handle the practically unimaginable pressure of medal competition? A simple, self-directed "You got this."

Such self-reassurance works equally well in the interpersonal arena. Get your bold on by reminding yourself of your capability, and then, similar to an athlete — or anyone — forging forward: "Just Do It." Research has demonstrated that throughout history, overconfident risk taking has proved much more advantageous than passivity. This assumes common sense, of course, as in don't attempt a black diamond run if you're a novice skier. Evolutionary psychologists (those who study cognitive and behavioral adaptations to changing environments) explain that overconfidence increases ambition and persistence, often eliciting a self-fulfilling prophecy leading to positive outcomes. So, yes, by all means do make a play for that crush you've been fantasizing about, or *you* ask the shy or inexperienced guy out for the second date, sometimes even the first for that matter. Think about the worst that can happen: if he doesn't respond or says no, all that's really lost is an abstract hope. In this circumstance, as in many other varied realms of life, there is so much more to gain than lose by taking action.

Finally, although the Internet has served as a mostly positive dating game changer when it comes to accessing new men, social media in particular also has a darker side in how it impacts self-esteem and confidence. Specifically, to avoid a self-inflicted, self-esteem hit, stop comparing your life to the posts and pics of your online friends; I guarantee it will never live up to those mostly idealized versions of reality. (Especially those posts that are nonstop-over-the-top.) Backing up my observations, a 2014 study out of the University of Houston found that heavy Facebook users who admitted that they were comparing themselves to friends experienced more depressive symptoms than those who logged less time on the site. Even before the study came out, psychologists referred to this self-defeating behavior as "compare and despair." I call it a complete confidence crash.

And then there's your own posting: within social media's never-ending parade of self-promotion, facts are often digitally whitewashed the way pictures are Photoshopped. In fact, I see many women in my practice who treat their dating life as though it is one big status update; they become more concerned about how their relationships appear to others than what they are actually feeling. To dodge this psychological black hole, as well as the aforementioned compare-and-despair syndrome, take a break from posting your dating details altogether, and, equally importantly, stop studying everyone else's. You'll feel much better about yourself as you focus more on what is really going on inside of you alone, rather than you in relation to your friends, online or otherwise.

An unexpected benefit of your own online behavior modification may be that you manage to preempt a looming social media addiction. Remarkably, research increasingly suggests that we get a jolt of dopamine, the brain's extremely pleasurable, rewarding neurotransmitter, when someone "likes" our Facebook or Instagram posts, or retweets our Twitter posts. Studies conducted at universities in Wales and Milan also show that heavy online media users suffer a "comedown" similar to that of drug users when they stop, which explains why you may have had trouble remaining offline and breaking an addiction you never even knew you had!

Optimism

A close cousin to confidence is optimism. If you're searching for an attitudinal magic bullet, then optimism is it. In recent years, psychological research and neuroscience together have credibly demonstrated that optimism, or the expectation of positive outcomes, is one of the most important requisites for happiness and contentment and is also linked to good health and longevity. For example, an especially rigorous 2011 study conducted by cognitive neuroscientist Sara Bengtsson, PhD, using task-relevant, self-concept labels such as "clever" and "stupid," revealed through functional magnetic resonance imaging (fMRI) that brains that don't expect good results fail to learn from their mistakes and improve over time. The "clever" woman who applies such findings to relationships gives herself a stratospheric advantage.

Takes the case of Meghan, a sweet, pretty twenty-eight-year-old dental hygienist. Each time she went out with a new guy, she told the entire sordid story of how her last two boyfriends had cheated on her, most recently with her younger sister. Not only was Meghan sharing TMI right from the start, but she also expected the new men to treat her poorly. They didn't prove her wrong. However, once Meghan optimistically convinced herself during therapy that she was going to find the positive, fulfilling relationship she deserved, Michael "magically" stepped into her life. It didn't hurt that Meghan finally set up expectations for respect and loyalty right from the start and didn't accept being taken for granted. Meghan reports that Michael still tells her daily how beautiful she is — four years into their marriage.

Specifically, women who expect to be successful with men generally are, no matter how long it takes. This is because expectations become self-fulfilling by influencing our actions, typically in an active, forward-moving direction, ultimately effecting favorable results. (Yes, this dynamic is very similar to that of overconfidence discussed above.) In other words, if you expect a good outcome in a particular undertaking, you'll be more likely to make that happen. As such, optimism is highly inspiring, motivating, and especially invaluable in the context of dating, where the hope of a happy experience allows women to risk getting to know a new man and, later, lay it all on the line — emotionally and physically.

Optimism is also the mechanism that allows women to continue to hang in there — and eventually find that someone special — even after a string of really bad dates or regrettable relationships with total jerks. (Think: guys who break up with you via email or text or, worse yet, by ignoring all of yours.) In this sense, the notion of the hopeless romantic might more accurately, and optimistically, be termed "hopeful romantic" instead. Regardless of terminology, successful outcomes of optimism abound. For example, even those who've gone through the bitterest of divorces often happily remarry. As British writer Samuel Johnson wryly remarked in 1776, "Marriage may be the ultimate triumph of hope over experience."

It's actually hopefulness within reason that's key; meaning you don't have to be an overly positive Pollyanna to reap the motivating aspects of optimism. Even a neutral attitude, however, is psychologically healthier than chronic negativity. Nevertheless, if you tend to be a not-so-perky pessimist, don't fret. Optimism, like confidence, can be cultivated. Begin practicing optimism by looking at the positive side of things — the "half-full" versus "half-empty" cup, and catch yourself each and every time you begin to slide into a doom-and-gloom mindset. Not only will you eventually become a much better problem solver, but you'll find yourself automatically meeting many of your dating and larger life challenges with optimism and resiliency. Talk about stronger!

Mindfulness in Dating

While confidence and optimism focus largely on beliefs and expectations, the practice of mindfulness in dating primarily involves attentiveness and awareness. The quintessential quality of mindfulness is a purposeful, present-centered, nonjudgmental awareness. The mindfulness movement, which essentially represents a melding of Buddhist practices with cognitive-behavioral psychology, gained considerable traction in the United States approximately twenty years ago. Its practice was consistently demonstrated to improve people's mental health and quality of life.

Mindfulness entails being fully present without thinking of the past or future. If practiced correctly, it lends a remarkable state of calm. The antithesis of mindfulness is "being in one's head" constantly, which I refer to as "head tripping." At its most benign, head tripping distracts from fleeting but potentially memorable moments in daily existence. And at its worst, in addition to exacerbating stress-related conditions such as migraine headaches and all sorts of skin breakouts, being "lost" in one's head leads people to effectively miss out on parts of their own lives. Here's a clear example of that from Nora Ephron's autobiographical *I Remember Nothing and Other Reflections*: "I went to many legendary rock concerts and spent them wondering when they would end and where we would eat afterward and whether the restaurant would still be open and what I would order. . . . On some level, my life has been wasted on me. After all, if I can't remember it, who can?"

When a woman practices mindfulness on a date, she is truly present, or "in" the moment, without any intrusive thoughts. She isn't worrying about anything else, such as what the guy thinks of her or whether or not he's going to ask her out for the weekend. Or that presentation she has to prepare for or her kid's parent-teacher conference. She isn't judging her date. Mindfulness also requires that you "lose" your iPhone for a few hours or so—listening to voicemails or reading texts or taking calls when you're out together mostly makes a man feel like everything/everyone else is more important. And really, isn't that the case? Practicing mindfulness not only enhances your experience of the date itself, it fosters reciprocal interest and communication. Furthermore, by being particularly attentive to *him* (try to focus more on the dude than the food), you won't miss subtle, but vital, signals that serve to bond people and cultivate emotional intimacy. Additionally, mindfulness lends an aura of openness and curiosity, a psychologically desirable attribute in both sexes.

You can achieve mindfulness only by blocking out miscellaneous distractions — whether in the room or in your head. Of course, this is easier said than done. However, one way to become adept at mindfulness is to practice approximately ten minutes of meditation (focusing on one thing only) daily through yoga, prayer, "silent-awareness," or even that exercise "zone "for example. Interestingly, according to an eighty-year longitudinal study out of Duke University, this practice is also a common attribute of people who rate themselves happiest. (Perhaps not so coincidentally, so is having a dog, which also tends to pull people into the present.) Happiness as a significant mental health benefit is reason alone to practice mindfulness, even without the added relationship perks such as increased intimacy and mental clarity.

Any hard-won brain gain, however, can easily be wiped out with two or three tequila shots or a few glasses of wine. Because alcohol has a depressive or restrictive effect on the brain's higher functioning, it "numbs" people to the realities of the moment, the exact *opposite* of mindful awareness. As a clinician, patients have always discussed drinking issues with me, both benign and serious in nature. However, drinking problems of young women in particular have recently taken on a new "twist": the women can't have sex without first getting drunk, but even then they rarely enjoy the experience. In essence, they are distancing themselves from the moment — and their partners — to engage in "polite," people-pleasing sex that they mistakenly assume is expected of them. This is not all that different from the sex workers whom I counsel, particularly erotic dancers and (former) call girls, who use alcohol and drugs before performing sex acts on and with men they find repulsive. But instead of women who society generally shuns and who are typically from abusive and/or impoverished backgrounds, these are young women of privilege from caring families.

These women, in fact, are very similar to University of Pennsylvania undergraduates interviewed at length about their sexual proclivities, with the findings discussed in a July 2013 *New York Times* article titled "Sex on Campus: She Can Play That Game, Too." As journalist Kate Taylor notes, "Women said universally that hookups could not exist without alcohol, because they were for the most part too uncomfortable to pair off with men they did not know well without being drunk." Taylor continues, "One girl, explaining why her encounters freshman and sophomore year often ended with fellatio, said that usually by the time she got back to a guy's room, she was starting to sober up and didn't want to be there anymore, and giving the guy oral sex was an easy way to wrap things up and leave."

More recently, *New York Times* journalists Jessica Bennett and Daniel Jones asked college students worldwide for their stories of navigating sexual consent, which were published in May, 2018. Alcohol also figures prominently in many of the narratives comprising the resultant "45 Stories of Rape and Consent on Campus." For example, coed Danni describes a hookup that included "recoiling" from her partner, whose last name she said she didn't even know at the time. As Danni recounted: "My mind, buried somewhere under layers of intoxication, finally figured that if I did it, I would get to go home, and no one would be mad at me."

In attempting to numb themselves to the anxiety and other unsettling feelings and thoughts provoked by their sexual encounters, young women are operating much as sex workers do to get through the day — except without the pay. (Note to men: don't consider buying a woman drinks as sexual currency.) And women, you shouldn't have to "leave" your body to give of your body; no matter how far along or out of hand a situation may seem, it's *always* okay to back out. (More on that later.)

Enthusiasm

Every few months, a version of the "same" patient walks into my office. She is a very attractive woman in her twenties, thirties, forties, or, increasingly, fifties and sixties, who is depressed because there is presently no special man in her life. The patient explains how she has always "needed" to be with a man to be happy but hates that she feels that way.

In one sense, the patient is being too hard on herself inasmuch as people share a universal predilection for lives infused with intimacy, love, and sex. It's no wonder that those urgings grow even stronger for women who may seek the added joyfulness and stability a great relationship provides. That said, women who strive for a partner to *enhance* their lives rather than *define* their lives tend to be become less discouraged and depressed during those "dry" or man-less periods. For instance, it's so empowering to wake up each morning and say to yourself: "I'm going to embrace the day," or "I'm going to kick butt today," whether or not you happen to be dating anyone special, or even anyone at all. (Side note: to kick butt you first need to get your feet out of bed.) Thinking longer-term, enthusiasm requires accepting the cards in life that we're dealt, playing them the best we can — and striving to win at one's *own* game of life, regardless.

Notably, the hit book *The Secret* variously refers to a "secret law of attraction" as a "law" of: "magnetic thoughts," "love," and "life," to name just a few of the many definitions included. It really is no "secret," however, that a person's positive attitude along with zest for life makes her responsible for her own happiness and attracts others to her as well. Likewise, any guy (other than a narcissist) who is upbeat and active in his own right will find it easier to be with a woman who brings her own passions and pastimes into the partnership, versus someone whose sole source of pleasure seems to be, well, him. Regarding the power of attitude, it has also been demonstrated that putting on a good face (for example, during a letdown outing or date) makes us feel better about a bad experience afterward. Not surprisingly, it's women (and men) who are hard to please and are easily jaded or bored who actually come across as most unpleasant and boring themselves.

In fact, enthusiasm is actually boredom's nemesis, relating to how you choose to spend, or perhaps more accurately how you have to spend your time. Notably, women's life satisfaction has been steadily declining the past few decades—undoubtedly due in part to increased stress or dissatisfaction with the way we're prioritizing our time. That fact alone warrants reflection on daily routines (while hopefully mitigating at least some *self-imposed* pressures that mostly just drive you crazy). What's important is that you find yourself engaged and excited about life in general. Underlining this statement, a 2007 Harvard study found that emotional vitality—"a sense of enthusiasm, of hopefulness, of engagement in life, and the ability to face life's stresses with emotional balance"—even reduced the risk of coronary heart disease. This scientific approach to attitude's far-reaching impact provides stark contrast to an easily misinterpreted expression being tossed around a lot lately in pop psychology: "Be interested *and* interesting."

Consider the following example. One of my patients, Ben, a forty-four-year-old cardiac surgeon, described meeting a very pretty private investigator during a homicide investigation at the hospital where he works. Ben, an avid *CSI* fan who has always been intrigued by detective work, initially was "over the moon" when the woman agreed to go out with him. However, once he and his Nancy Drew actually started dating, he was quickly put off by her sullen demeanor and apathetic attitude. Needless to say, the relationship was short lived. But three months later Ben met a warm, enthusiastic single mother/homemaker. He presently reports being "head over heels in love with [her]." Ben's experience suggests that a woman's profession need not be the only thing making her interesting or appealing; it's her passion and enthusiasm with which she engages in her world, regardless of job title.

One final note: reaffirming your own core values about life and love will additionally help you muster the strength to leave a somehow compelling but ultimately toxic, vitality-zapping man—many of whom will be described in the next Step. And, equally important, you'll gain (or restore) the confidence to seek a relationship where you're deeply valued by your partner, perhaps for the first time.

Step 2 Playlist ♫
You Gotta Be/Des'ree
Flawless/Beyoncé
Stronger/Brittany Spears

I might have saved a little trouble for the next girl
'Cause the next time that he cheats
Oh, you know it won't be on me
—Carrie Underwood

Step 3

Hard Truths: All About Men (and Which to Avoid)

*L*ynn is a young-looking fifty-two-year-old, newly divorced mother of three who currently finds herself "madly in love" with her thirty-four-year-old personal trainer. She claims that he feels the same way about her, too, but is worried because he wants to start a family. At the other extreme, there's Katie, a twenty-four-year-old makeup artist, who is about to move in with her forty-five-year-old rock star (really, an enormously successful musician). Katie's boyfriend, by the way, cheated on her once — that she knows of — and has two failed marriages behind him. Both patients have asked me whether their relationships can survive.

My answer: not likely.

Men's Passages (Including the Midlife Crisis)

As a clinical psychologist, I'm frequently asked for my opinion regarding whether a man is "too old" or, increasingly, "too young" for a woman to date.

Age difference does, in fact, affect compatibility, but at the risk of begging the question, it depends largely on how old someone is. Notably, while a person's true character generally doesn't change much over time, life experience and maturation does change people in other ways, sometimes unrecognizably.

The following chart, titled "Men's Emotional Maturation," is meant as a general guideline of adult men's stages of life with important implications for dating. Each decade is defined with a Major Developmental Descriptor (MDD) that captures the neuropsychological essence of those years; for example, men in their teens are neurologically wired to be the most impulsive, so the MDD for the teenage years is "impulsivity." Men must also resolve a primary psychological challenge in each decade before they can "pass" to the next stage of life. What this means is that a thirty-one-year-old man may be developmentally "stuck" in his twenties, for example, if he hasn't yet gained a sense of independence. In addition to drawing heavily from the field of neuropsychology, the norms proposed are also informed by shared confidences of men of all ages and walks of life, a group that over the years includes patients, boyfriends, friends, random acquaintances, husband (one so far), and of course, my two grown sons.

MEN'S EMOTIONAL MATURATION

Chronological Age	Major Developmental Descriptor (MDD)	Psychological Challenge
Teens	Impulsivity	Fitting In
Twenties	Peak Performance	Independence
Thirties	Stability	Charting Life Course
Forties	Mastery	Happiness
Fifties	Maintenance	Connection
Sixties	Adaptation	Relevance

The smart woman who understands what makes men tick is a far better dating—and life—partner. So here's the real rundown on how a man's chronological age and the psychological challenges he faces influence his choice of women and approach to relationships. Once you understand "normal" (technically normative) guy behavior, you'll be ready for the next section on emotionally dangerous outliers, or which Men to Avoid.

Teens

If you're a young woman who's dating a teenage guy (presumably but not necessarily in his late teens), then it's important to be aware of how impulsive he can be. For instance, a guy whom you're making out with at a party may abruptly go from heavy kissing and petting to asking if he can "put it in." (Yes, that happened to one of my high school patients.) Compromised judgment adds to the problem because the area of the brain responsible for judgment, reasoning, and the moderation of social behavior (the prefrontal cortex) isn't fully developed in adolescence. Teenage boys also desperately want to fit in with their peers; if their friends are having sex, then they'll strive to emulate them. So while you may be thinking of your Teen Dream as a romantic hero of sorts, having intercourse with you mostly makes him feel more like a hero among his bros. Similarly, with some especially immature, insecure guys you run the risk of becoming a mere vehicle for bragging rights. Because the adolescent Adonis tends to act on immediate impulses, it will be up to you to rein him in. Similarly, due to his poor judgment, your heartthrob may not consider the consequences of his actions; therefore, typically you also will be the one who needs to bear the burden of thinking ahead, especially regarding potential STDs and pregnancy. If all this sounds like an enormous responsibility — it is. But don't despair, little sister: things dramatically improve for you as dudes mature into their twenties.

Twenties

For men (as well as women), the human brain is not fully developed until age twenty-six. This is because myelin sheaths, which are insular material allowing for proper functioning of the nervous system, aren't fully formed until then. Essentially, a man reaches his peak level of intellectual and physical functioning in his late and early twenties, respectively. So a twenty-nine-year-old's decision-making process will generally be much more solid than at twenty-one.

While decisions and choices vary, the twentysomething-year-old man approaches relationships from a position of continually increasing confidence and independence. Also, when it comes to girls, men in their twenties are, compared with their older cohorts, guileless. Meaning that they have a certain idealistic innocence and genuine romantic spirit that hasn't yet been beaten down by life. Twentysomethings show more and more decisiveness in various pursuits (including the pursuit of *you*), as they assert their independence. Which makes it very possible for you to meet your future husband when he's in his twenties. However, if you both are in your early twenties, it may not be the wisest decision to irrevocably choose a lifelong partner before your brains are (literally) all there.

That is not to say that marriages between twenty-two-year-olds cannot be successful; they certainly can be, as innumerable married couples who tied the knot early on will attest. But to prevent that happily tight knot from becoming a nuptial noose, both partners have to be ready to weather many more changes in themselves and each other than when marrying later. Furthermore, the likelihood of a twentysomething male seeking a committed relationship increases as he approaches his late twenties. According to US Census Bureau statistics, the average age of first marriage for men is twenty-seven years old. The twentysomething male typically takes even bigger strides toward the altar as he moves through his early thirties.
(Side note: the word "altar" is derived from the Latin practice of ritualistic sacrifice. Just sayin'.)

Thirties

If you happen to be a woman who is "going for the gold" — in this case a golden wedding band — the guy in his thirties is your man! Developmentally, he has reached a point in his life where he strives for security and stability both professionally and in his relationships. Similarly, men in their early to mid-thirties begin to think very seriously about what they want their futures to look like; what's more, they take definitive action toward realizing their vision. Therefore, a man in his thirties who has decided that he eventually wants kids and a family will try very hard to find his "person" to make that happen. In contrast, although the twentysomething man may have the same long-term goals, he views them with less urgency.

Whether a dreamer or a doer (preferably both), men in their thirties often seek meaning in their lives; planning a family sometimes offers a handy solution. And even when men don't want children, they hit thirtysomething and decide it's time to settle down. Very frequently when I encounter an engaged couple, the man is in his thirties. Likewise, if anyone were ever to quantify the modal number, or the most common age at which college-educated American men become engaged for the first time, I'd surmise it to be thirty-two, which I refer to as the "sweet spot" of dating. It follows that if you have a thirty-two-year-old non-narcissistic, long-term boyfriend, your chances are very good that he will be a keeper.

Unless you're Lynn, the divorced fifty-two-year-old mom mentioned previously who's involved with her thirty-four-year-old trainer, Chad. Lynn describes Chad as "*so* attentive" and "beyond fantastic." But he's already picked out names for his as yet unborn kids; clearly an indication of Psychological Challenge "planning for future." Sadly, given their markedly different life passages, Chad's future most likely won't include Lynn.

Forties

In contrast to men in their thirties who look outward toward the future, a fortysomething-year-old man will invariably look inward. He likely has already achieved a level of mastery with regard to his job and relationships, so he will now have the newfound freedom to ask himself the question, "Am I truly happy?" This is also what is popularly referred to as the "midlife crisis." However, such inward searching is actually a time of psychological reckoning, rather than a crisis, which has an inherently negative connotation. (In reality, much too often a mid-lifer's "reckoning" results in a true crisis mainly for those closest to him.) This is when otherwise happily married men short on integrity engage in extramarital affairs while rationalizing that they need their paramours or mistresses to fulfill a need left fallow by their wives (who themselves may be on a never-ending merry-go-round of exhausting job stressors, household chores, child care, etc.). The husbands' self-serving rationalization typically distorts reality and forms the foundation for a web of trust-shattering lies.

Also, if you happen to be a woman in your twenties who is involved with a fortysomething-year-old man, beware that what makes him happy now (bragging rights to dating a much younger woman; newish, exciting sex) will invariably change as he enters his fifties, yielding a change in the women he seeks out as well. Even if you're close to his own age, it may be surprisingly difficult to get your fortysomething-year-old partner to commit to something as permanent as marriage. This is because the fortysomething-year-old man's psychological frame of reference keeps pointing back to his *own* happiness (including what you "bring to the table"), instead of your overall viability as a couple. Nevertheless, if he perceives that you fit into his image of what a happy life looks like, you have a much better chance of becoming that "perfect" second wife, even if you end up as his first.

Fifties

Whereas men in their forties tend to be masters of their universes, they unfortunately are not immune to encroaching changes that inevitably arrive with time. As men advance through their fifties and beyond, they begin to notice a subtle, insidious decline in both their intellectual and physical capabilities. For example, short-term memory may not be as sharp as it previously was (one of my patients even forgot to pack a pair of dress trousers for a trip with foreign dignitaries). This is the period when men's bodies also begin to show signs of aging, with diminished muscle strength and arthritic joints, or both. As hormone production and testosterone bioavailability gradually decline, men in their fifties may also begin to experience decreased energy and changes in mood. These hormonal changes are typically accompanied by diminished virility with regard to psychosexual drive (libido), as well as varying degrees of difficulty initiating and sustaining erectile function.

The Major Developmental Descriptor assigned to men in their fifties is "maintenance," as they attempt to maintain a sense of mental and physical integrity in the face of aging. Hence, there is the fiftysomething-year-old who fights hard against the biological clock by continuing to pursue or reengage in professionally and physically demanding activities determined to prove to himself (and everyone else) that he is just as fit as in his younger years. And sometimes even more so: consider the sharp, vibrant fiftysomething guy who comes off on top of the world mentally, physically — and romantically. Notably, modern medicine has enabled elder Romeos with increasing erectile issues to also keep up their stamina (so to speak!) in the bedroom through the development of drugs such as Viagra and Cialis.

It follows from the fiftysomething-year-old man's developmental decline that his major psychological challenge is connection: he seeks not only a connection to his former strong, capable self, but also to people. If your fiftyish male partner is divorced, you may witness him newly reaching out to young adult children who are just leaving home or otherwise establishing their own independence. Still, he's glad they're grown. In fact, some men with older children prefer to date childless women because "they don't want to go through it all again." However, many fiftysomething fathers like to date women who are mothers themselves, because they believe that these women will understand their commitment to their kids better than childless women.

This was clearly evidenced in the case of a forty-eight-year-old, never-married female patient who was dating a fifty-five-year-old widower with three teenage kids. In therapy Laura described how she had continually made a point of fawning over her partner's children, claiming how she "couldn't wait" to be a mom to them. Part of the problem (besides pushing the guy to become serious before he was ready) was that she was disingenuous. Laura's boyfriend picked up on the falseness, perhaps because she became upset whenever, as she put it, he "chose his kids over her." The guy abruptly broke up with my patient (the impetus for therapy) and became engaged the following year to a divorced mother of four. Laura would have been much better off supporting his role as a dad rather than feigning feelings that she didn't have. Regardless of whether you've raised kids or not, if you can help your midlife mate reaffirm the best of who he is, you are well on your way to becoming a permanent fixture in his life. At the very least, his powerful need to connect with people bodes well for a strong romantic connection with you.

Sixties

The sixtysomething-year-old man, in contrast to his decade-younger self, is no longer unduly alarmed by the changes accompanying the aging process. Rather, he accepts and makes the most of such changes, leading to the Major Developmental Descriptor for the years from sixty through sixty-nine of "adaptation." The word, which originates from the Latin *adaptare*, meaning "to fit," denotes a positive adjustment or modification to changing conditions. Things finally come together for the *well-adjusted* sixtysomething-year-old man who reaps the rewards of all those efforts he's already made second nature. For example, as noted, men in their fifties often "rebel" against diminished muscle tone by aggressively seeking out physically demanding hobbies or sports. In contrast, a sixty-five-year-old may be just as active as ever because he's incorporated exercise into his lifestyle, not because he's trying to prove anything. Also, although he's not necessarily slowing down, an increasing awareness of his own mortality may lead the sixtysomething-year-old man to indulge in more respites or vacations that he'd previously denied himself. Coincidentally, just as I was musing that barring serious illness, older folks tend to be much calmer and more contented than twentysomething-year-old stressed, depressed cohorts, Gallup poll research was published in the August, 2016 *Journal of Clinical Psychology* showing that people become happier as they age.

For that happiness to continue well into one's sixties and beyond, however, men (and women as well) need to feel "relevant" to others, whether professionally or personally. Meaning that they want to know that they still matter despite the myriad changes that inevitably come with the passage of time. Philosophically, consider this as twenty-first century "senior" existential angst. Paul McCartney, a modern-day Socrates of sorts, conveys the psychological challenge of men in their sixties best with the iconic question, "Will you still need me, will you still feed me, when I'm sixty-four?" (Surprisingly, McCartney wrote these prescient lyrics in 1958, when he was just sixteen years old.) Yes, even aging rock icons need reassurance every now and then—and so does your sexagenarian soul mate.

Men to Avoid

No matter their age, there are many men who, simply put, are trouble. And I don't mean "trouble" as in benign-bad-boy trouble. Rather, I'm talking about tear-your-heart-out trouble.

The question to ask yourself if you're involved with any of these men is: Does having this person intimately in my life make me happier than being without him, even though I know I'll never get what I really want? If so, then welcome to the human (nay, female) condition. Just prepare to inoculate yourself against the frequent disappointments, and brace yourself for the inevitable future free fall. Also, don't let your involvement with any of the following men keep you from searching for other dating prospects who can give you the truly loving partnership you want and deserve. Most important, be smart and aware, and don't delude yourself. If your partner is unable or unwilling to fill your needs in a relationship, it's time to find someone who can.

Men Who Are Trouble

- Commitment-phobes
- Serial philanderers
- Newly divorced men with minimal premarital sexual experience
- Emotional manipulators
- Players
- Narcissists
- Unreachables
- "Separated" husbands

Here's the breakdown:

Commitment-phobes

These men truly are into you, but the idea of any sort of commitment freaks them out. Meaning that they are overtaken by irrational fear and/or disabling anxiety at the mere thought of engagement or marriage. With anyone. Fortunately, these guys are actually rare: normal trepidation notwithstanding, most men actually do want to commit to a woman they're in love with when the timing is right.

Serial Philanderers

The words "loyalty" and "trust" are conspicuously missing from the serial philanderer's vocabulary, as well as from his life. Unlike the player, whose primary motivation is sexual gratification outside the confines of a long-term relationship, the serial philanderer often sincerely seeks commitment. From you, that is. The problem is this guy has a wandering eye and can't keep his pants on. Regardless of how much he may love or care for his partner. One proposed psychological theory to explain serial philandering, a form of compulsive sexual behavior, is that it's due to an "addiction" akin to a drug addiction where the person can't stop a highly rewarding behavior despite grossly negative personal consequences. However, it's notable that compulsive sexual behavior didn't make the cut as an addiction in the newest, revised edition of *The Diagnostic and Statistical Manual of Mental Disorders (DSM)* (the mental health profession's bible).

In addition to aggressive serial cheating where men in monogamous relationships surreptitiously seek out sexual hookups, there's the more passive opportunistic guy who caves to temptation — make that nearly every attractive temptation. (It's important to differentiate serial cheating from the guy who cheats just once, usually out of opportunity, but is genuinely remorseful and, perhaps most important, capable of stopping.) Regardless of what causes it, your partner's continual straying is extremely hurtful to you. Typically the serial philanderer has a string of broken relationships due to his cheating.

Going back to the relationship between Katie and her rock star boyfriend who admitted to cheating on her once; it became evident that his track record (no harmony here) of sleeping around was actually what destroyed his former marriages. Which means that Katie is far more likely to find herself in yet another of her boyfriend's gold albums (perhaps about love gone wrong) than in his golden years.

Newly Divorced: It Depends

Here is where the circumstances of the divorce are key. Generally, a very successful, wealthy, or otherwise prominent man who leaves his wife primarily because he is no longer "in love" with her is a poor dating risk. This guy suffers from "single-envy": what he actually is in love with is the idea of sexual freedom. Especially if he had minimal or no premarital sexual experience. So now he can compensate for never having dated the proverbial popular cheerleader, because his money will buy her. Yes, the vapid women he meets will grow tiresome, and he eventually will settle down with a younger, shinier version of his former wife. But it's very difficult to predict when.

Emotional Manipulators

These are perhaps the most damaging of the bunch so far because it's difficult to realize that something is very wrong until you're well into the relationship. Essentially, emotional manipulators are consistently dismissive of your needs and feelings, and often condescending, but just engaged enough to keep you from leaving. They take no responsibility for frequent self-serving lies; when caught in one they often continue to deny or distort the truth while somehow blaming you. Similarly, when you attempt to stand up for yourself, this cunning operator will often falsely accuse you of being "mean" or "criticizing" him. Other common tactics employed by the emotional manipulator include chilly—and chilling—silences, constant criticism, frequent threats, button-pushing, intimate abandonment (a.k.a. no sex), and changing the meaning of words. (The latter is when someone insists you said or meant something you didn't, also referred to as "putting words in one's mouth.") Stonewalling, or the categorical refusal to accept any perspective other than their own, is also very common. Equally devastating, the emotional manipulator's nasty communications are frequently accompanied by cut-to-the-core mean, contemptuous looks and body language. For these reasons, sorry Pink, but no matter how many instances we get up and "try," emotional manipulators will burn—no, make that scorch—us every time.

Players

A player will deliberately seduce you into thinking he cares—and into bed—when all he really cares about is his own sexual gratification. For example, in a groundbreaking collaborative study conducted by David Buss, PhD, at the University of

Texas–Austin and Marie Haselton, PhD, at UCLA, it was found that the greater number of previous sexual partners a man has had, the more quickly he will perceive unattractiveness in a woman after first intercourse. What this means is that a player, defined as a man whose primary dating goals are sexual, will do what it takes to sleep with you before soon devaluing you and moving on to someone else. In contrast to a casual hookup where at least the guy is upfront about wanting sex, a player will string you along with your heart on a leash for a few weeks or even months just so he's still having a good time. The millennial version of a player is the so-called "softboy" who knows exactly how to tug on your heartstrings before abruptly letting go. You're left agonizing over what went wrong when you never really had a chance from the start. (See also: Why He Doesn't Call, Step 8)

Narcissists

Similar to players are narcissistic men, who, while not necessarily unscrupulous, can also be difficult as they are primarily concerned about themselves and their image. In fact, you may initially be attracted by a narcissist's oftentimes good looks and veneer of power or wealth. Also, please do note that a bit of narcissism, which is expressed as playfulness and charm, is universally appealing. However, if the narcissism is over the top, then consider it a blessing in disguise that you are no longer dating this Prince of His Own Kingdom. Involvement with a pathological narcissist will send a woman on a path to almost certain grief, particularly because of his lack of empathy and out-of-control entitlement (i.e., unreasonable expectations of automatic compliance with his demands, whether by you, or even a server in a restaurant). Notably, a defining characteristic of narcissism is insensitivity to the feelings of others, which no amount of charm can ever compensate for, especially in a serious relationship.

One early warning sign that you are dating a narcissist is if he discusses *his* issues in inappropriately lengthy detail while being impatient, irritated, dismissive, and/or altogether ignoring when you try to talk about your own concerns. Similarly, it won't be long before you are taken aback (at the very least) by his emotional coldness and lack of reciprocal interest. Even if they are finally recognized, your needs and feelings will likely be disparagingly written off as "proof" that you're "needy." But, as the *DSM* explains, that doesn't stop the narcissist from continuing to fish for compliments from you, or from anyone else for that matter. Add that to the fact that narcissists don't take criticism well, as in they may rage and defiantly counterattack. In a similar vein, narcissists rarely apologize because they can't ever admit they're wrong. So if all this sounds like your guy, who also grossly exaggerates his achievements and talents — constantly — then I have only two words for your relationship: *get out*.

Unreachables

Do you ever watch *Dateline* mysteries where the girlfriend/ wife ends up murdered at the hands of her boyfriend/husband? (Typically there is a love triangle and/or hefty life insurance policy involved.) At first the couple seems "perfectly happy" — until one day she's found with a knife in her throat, or pushed off a cliff. What nearly all these women have in common early on in the relationship's souring is seemingly minor but oh so telling: they often can't reach their partner on his cell for hours on end, with his whereabouts unaccounted for. Texts are ignored, and voice messages are left unanswered; the concern, anxiety, and sometimes panic in the woman's voice unheeded. And if the "unreachable" does bother to phone back at all, it's usually not until several hours later, with some BS reason given for his disappearance.

At first, thirty-six-year-old Anne didn't think much about it when she couldn't reach her live-in partner at least two or three days each week from late afternoon until well into the night. After all, her physician-boyfriend always had a ready explanation for his constant disappearances: Medical meetings went late. A patient had an emergency. There was no cell reception in the hospital where he was catching up on charts. Anne also learned to ignore her own common sense, which told her that the excuses didn't add up (e.g., no medical meetings last past 1 a.m.). However, when she was six months pregnant and accidentally found a crack pipe tucked away in her then-fiancé's sunglass case (while searching for her own missing sunglasses), this Ivy League graduate finally realized what was going on.

If any of this sounds even remotely familiar, ask yourself whether your guy's unreliability has become a *repeated pattern;* anyone can go AWOL every once in a (long) while. But if you find yourself being greeted by that now-annoying outgoing message on his cell (instead of his real-time voice) far more often than you should — and dying a little inside each time you do — know that this is a very bad sign. While in all likelihood not a future murderer, your partner is at minimum deprioritizing you by his continual unavailability. And that's the least of it. His blatant indifference to your expressed need for minimal, respectful contact is unconscionable. Men who constantly "disappear" without good explanation could be doing anything: other women, drug or alcohol binges, etc. Don't be intimidated to ask him some hard questions; if you don't get straight answers, perhaps it's finally time for you to make yourself unreachable to him as well — except in your case, permanently.

"Separated" Husbands

Be very, very wary of the so-called love a separated man professes for you; although his feelings may be genuine, his promises in particular are likely to be broken. Especially when the guy decides that he actually doesn't want to overhaul his life. And let's not forget intentionally deceptive married men, separated or not. Regarding the latter category of reluctant husbands, please beware that lying isn't exclusive to single dudes. For example, I've recently seen two women in therapy whose married lovers went so far as to tell them that their wives had some vague form of quasi-terminal illness (read: long-term marriage). But the wives somehow made "amazing," "medicine-defying" full recoveries coincidentally just when my patients demanded more of the men. (Even if they weren't lying, the men's inclination to abandon ill spouses speaks to a disturbingly unapologetic lack of character — and conscience.) In fact, to avoid heartache all around (yours and everyone else's), consider anyone else's husband off-limits.

That is, if you even realize your love interest is someone else's husband. My patient, Natalie, was highly invested in a new man she'd been dating for a month who led her to believe he'd been divorced for several years; he even talked about a recent breakup with a long-term girlfriend. But upon returning from a weekend trip where they slept together for the first (and last) time, the guy finally fessed up that he was actually still *married*, but "lived separately," including romantic involvements, from his (conveniently) out-of-state wife.

Lying by omission seems to be an especially common tactic these days among both separated and fake-divorced men. And what you don't know actually *can* hurt you. So don't be afraid to ask any questions of him you need; it's better to risk being intrusive than it is to be intentionally deceived.

> *Here's to the hearts that ache, here's to the mess we make*
> — Mia, La La Land

I Should Have Known: Red Flags Lead OUT

Even armed with knowledge of men to avoid, many times there is simply no way to predict who will ultimately burn you. But if you start listening to your instincts early on, at least you stand a chance. It's primarily when women flat out disregard signals that are making them uneasy or uncomfortable that they run into trouble. Which is exactly what happened to the following two patients.

Amanda had been dating her boyfriend, Ryan, for well over a year; however, she realized something just didn't "feel right" all along. Particularly disconcerting was Ryan's cavalier manner of throwing huge amounts of cash around: Rodeo Drive shopping sprees, five-star hotels, thousands spent on bottle service, etc. Although Ryan claimed to be "in real estate," he was decidedly evasive when pressed for details. Always. Turns out Ryan's "work" involved an elaborate Ponzi scheme. Despite the ever-present arsenal of alarm signals, Amanda turned down a prestigious, out-of-state graduate school program to be with this con man. That's what manipulators do: without even entertaining the possibly of a long-distance relationship, he convinced an otherwise bright, accomplished young woman that her life would begin to crumble — without him — if she attended her dream school.

Or, take the case of thirty-one-year-old Sophia, who sought treatment with me because of her involvement with a high-profile politician she met through work who had become controlling to the point that he chose her outfits each time they went out. He also countered any initiative Sophia took, even refusing to dine at restaurants he liked if she did the choosing. Sophia's partner additionally "took charge" by repeatedly neglecting to consult her when booking expensive, nonrefundable theater tickets without checking whether the performances were of interest to her or if the dates were convenient. This political VIP also humiliated my patient publicly by making jokes at her expense; for instance, admonishing a group of campaign donors, "Don't ask Sophia's opinion because the only 'party' she's interested in is one where alcohol is served." Even so, when Sophia tried to break away from her abusive partner, he would coax her into staying in the relationship with apologies and gifts.

Sophia described how, upon first meeting this man, she had a "weird feeling" but was nevertheless flattered by the attention. She also ignored her instinct not to sleep with him immediately, instead allowing herself to be seduced by his money and power. Sophia finally did manage to break up with the guy, but not before she lost her job after he copied her coworkers on a rambling email she had previously sent him venting after a tough day at work. In the email, Sophia had criticized everything from her colleagues' choice of clothes to her supervisor's micromanaging. Once again, Sophia's instincts would have protected her from this emotional victimization right from the start had she paid attention.

Although Amanda's and Sophia's experiences are fairly extreme, some warning signs are far more common. For instance, say you're at a party with someone you've been dating for a while, and another guy hits on you. A "normal," caring man may get jealous but will respond with a comment like, "Hey, she's with me—she's gorgeous—and I know I'm a really lucky guy." However, a red flag indicator of a problematic partner would be one who somehow rages at the man for approaching you, and later angrily accuses you of standing too close, flirting, being too friendly, or otherwise insinuating that you provoked the attention. In this instance your partner is denying your inherent attractiveness, charisma, etc. by manipulatively blaming your actions for the incident. The operative words here are "angrily" and "manipulatively"; your partner's inappropriate outburst might be accounted for by being excessively possessive, controlling, or jealous. Or his angry tirade might be covertly drug-fueled or otherwise suggestive of a problem you didn't even know he had. Just like you wouldn't ignore a red flag on a beach and wade into dangerous waters, don't ignore the warning bells that are clamoring for attention in your head. All the bogus excuses for him you make (to yourself) can't hide what you know deep down: you desire and deserve a relationship steeped in joy and gratitude versus tears and fears.

Step 3 Playlist ♫
Before He Cheats/Carrie Underwood
Try/Pink
When I'm Sixty Four/Paul McCartney
Audition (The Fools Who Dream)/Justin Hurwitz, Benj Pasek, Justin Paul

Part 2:

IGNITING A ROMANTIC CONNECTION

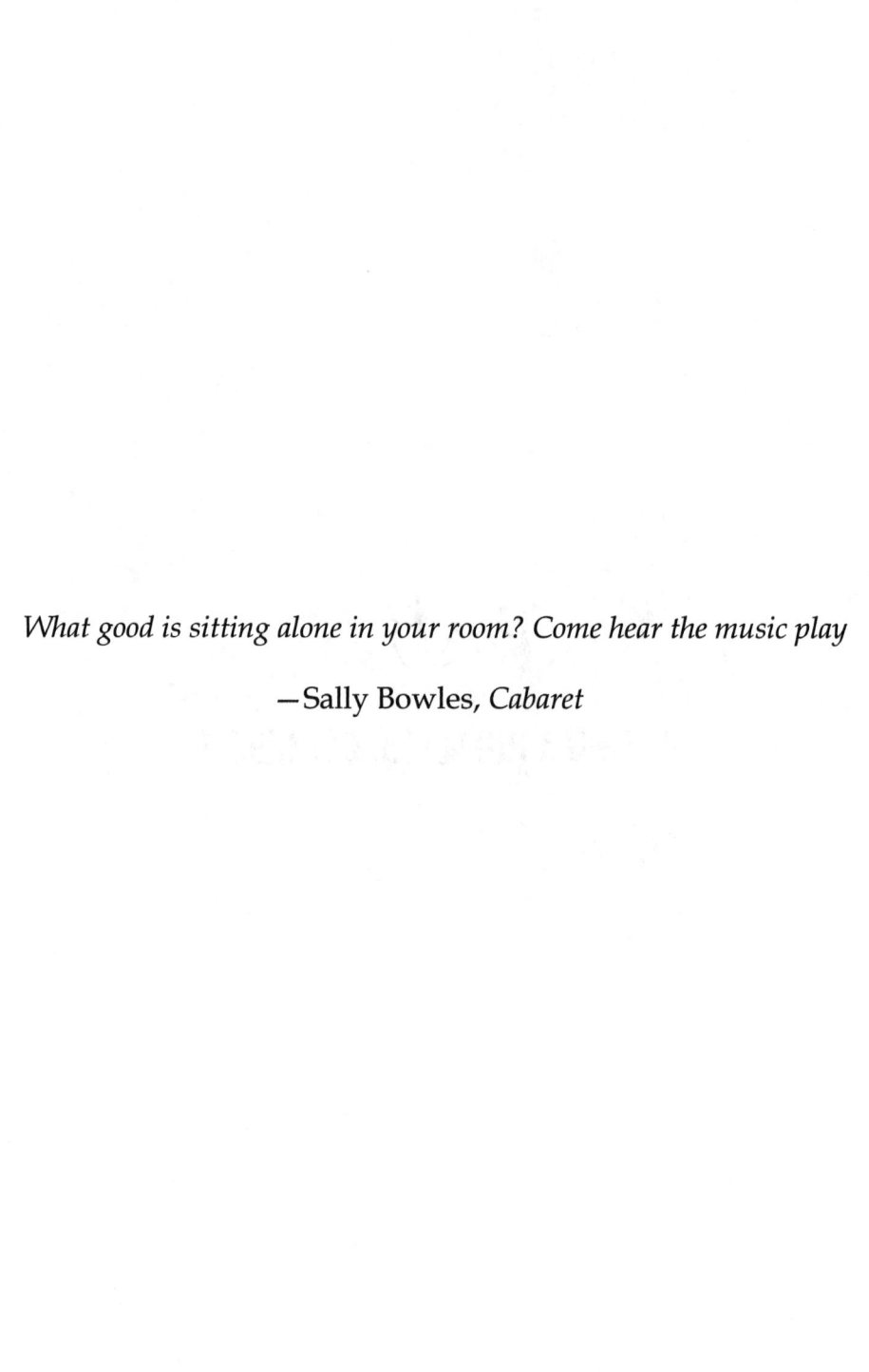

What good is sitting alone in your room? Come hear the music play

—Sally Bowles, *Cabaret*

Step 4

Finding Him: Step Out of
Your Comfort Zone

C hance, or fate, plays a huge role in the early stages of dating insofar as how couples meet. To illustrate the randomness of it all, I recently met an adorable, outgoing couple, Ron and Roz (real names), who have been happily married for sixty-nine years. When asked how they met, Ron exuberantly explained that they'd been standing in line next to one another their first day of UCLA at the registrar's office—and have been together ever since. (Including a day-after-graduation marriage.) Then there's the similarly serendipitous story of my patient, Nicole, who met her fiancé on a flight from Los Angeles to New York. She'd missed an earlier flight and wasn't even supposed to be on that one!

At the opposite end of life's capriciousness, two (well-suited) people could be invited to the same party or other social function but arrive and leave at different times such that they never meet one another. Or they could attend the same university and even take the same course, but be in different sections and never cross paths. Even Internet dating, which has an inherent degree of purposefulness and selectivity, is subject to chance in the timing of when any two people choose to go online.

Women additionally need to understand that the place or places they spend the most waking hours will also be where they'll meet men—hopefully single—to date. So if a woman works in female apparel, her dating prospects may be far more limited than a woman who works in finance (where the ratio of men to women is four to one). That doesn't mean that the fashion designer won't necessarily meet and become involved with an investment banker, but she has to venture outside her comfort zone and step up her game to do so. All too often, however, women become cocooned in their own limited lives and network groups and then are frustrated when there's nobody to date. Also, stop paying attention to depressing statistics that compare finding a good man to getting hit by lighting, especially after a certain age. Those statistics are taken out of context and manipulated in sensationalistic ways; all they really do is give men an inflated sense of their own importance and women an excuse for getting lazy. The key to Step 4 is to take control and increase the odds of finding a guy who is right for you by accessing as many potential dating partners as possible.

The Three Month Test

Here's a test: count back three months. Have you met a man face to face who has asked you out within those three months? (This doesn't include meeting someone online.) If your answer is yes, then your home turf is working well for you. By "home turf" I mean the place or places you spend most of your waking hours, such as school or work. (It can also literally mean home; one of my patients met her long-term boyfriend in the parking lot of their condominium building.) But perhaps you attend a commuter college with limited opportunities for socializing, or your workplace surrounds you with mostly married or gay men or—equally discouraging—no men at all. Then your answer to the question above would likely be no, and I'd further surmise that you haven't met any dating prospects at school or work even in the last six months or longer. If this is the case, then you definitely need to start thinking outside the box—and get out of your own self-imposed "box." So stop complaining that you aren't meeting any new men: *now* is the time to step up, step out, and give blind luck a hand.

New Ways to Meet Men

- Athletic groups such as hiking, running, volleyball, Masters swim, rowing
- Line, folk, salsa and square dancing
- Wine tasting events/wine bars
- Adult classes at local college/university
- Mensa
- Country club/hotel spa membership (Look for unpublicized discounts.)
- Civic, philanthropic or political groups
- Church/synagogue
- Organized events sponsored by local museums, shopping centers, libraries, etc.
- Meetup.com
- College alumni association

The same active planning and determination used in business to bring about a desired goal or find a solution to a problem also holds for one's personal life. To note, it's fairly obvious you're not going to achieve career advancement by sitting and waiting for that dream job to come to you. Applied socially, think about how to expand on your own interests, and then add new activities where you'd be likely to meet like-minded men. For example, if you're athletic consider joining: a local gym or sports club; Masters swim or rowing team; or running, hiking, or volleyball group. These are particularly excellent options for meeting someone because we tend to start conversations with the people we see over and over, as would likely be the case in these venues. Ditto for line dancing, as well as folk, salsa, and square dancing, which are all about vibing and connecting with others — on the dance floor as well as off.

Also, check out local wine tastings—but only if you can remain sober. People loosen up and tend to be receptive to talking to new people at these "civilized" bacchanalian events, which, in contrast to aimless barhopping, are more purposeful. As one wine-enthusiast friend of mine remarked, she's met more men who are *true* connoisseurs, versus those at bars who primarily wish to "connoisseur" her. And speaking of wine, take your Kindle or an engrossing book to a wine bar or other gathering spot with a friendly vibe. Your book provides an easy excuse for an interested guy to make an approach while you're sipping solo.

If you want to meet more men, that also means giving consistent, regularly scheduled new activities a fair shake. Are you out of school but love to learn? Sign up for an adult night class at a local college or university (even a local high school) where you'll meet others with similar pursuits. Are you a brainiac looking for an equally smart soul mate? You may wish to consider joining Mensa, a social organization whose admission is conditional on high IQ. Group activities listed on the organization's website range from weekend dinner and drinks to speakers, seminars, and "lively" discussions scheduled throughout the month.

Then again, if you're more material girl than Mensa material, you may meet your match at a local country club. Many such clubs offer unpublicized discounts to highly sought-after groups, young professionals for example. Similarly it's a well-kept secret that some yacht clubs and high-end hotels offer partial use of their facilities, including pool/spa access and classes (Yoga, sailing, etc.), through special programs for non-members/non-guests. If participation is consistent, you're bound to meet other local regulars (hopefully men) over time. The same is true of civic, philanthropic, and politically focused groups. Regardless of your chosen pastime, it's undisputable that when people share interests, they're much more likely to bond—and if "chemistry" cooperates, that's just the beginning.

Let's return to the scenario where your work leads you to interact mostly with other women, and ditto for your interests (for example, ballet). Or perhaps your job is simply solitary in nature. Consider checking out some of the "happening" clubs or restaurants in your neighborhood. Or even a strategically located coffee shop or deli. This doesn't have to be complicated. Emily, a thirty-three-year-old actress and freelance writer with standout looks and personality, came to me for assistance with both writer's block and relationship problems. It quickly became apparent that Emily needed to change her boyfriend just as badly, if not more so, than she did her workspace. So I suggested she set up shop somewhere other than her apartment, where she was continually distracted by her out-of-work, belligerent boyfriend (who also happens to be a problem drinker). Within weeks Emily bid adieu to the downer boyfriend and met a cra-zy-'bout-her Fortune 500 alpha male just by setting up a make-shift "office" (her laptop) at the coffee house downstairs from his company's offices. Her book, however, remains unfinished.

While the above "Starbucks-crossed" lovers truly met by chance, many of my patients have "helped" fate along. For example, Cheryl, a successful entrepreneur in her late forties, was upset about not meeting men who met her very stringent financial requirements. As in she wanted a zillionaire. After only two sessions on out-of-box thinking, Cheryl expanded her consulting business by offering services to corporate owners and executives. It took a degree of perseverance, but this buxom blonde finally found a VIP who sealed more than a business deal (including the escrow papers on *their* hillside dream house).

Also, by all means please don't overlook a friendly neighborhood church or synagogue because you have abandoned religion since your confirmation, bat mitzvah, or brachmach-arya (Hindu). Many such institutions schedule events for singles that can be an especially great way to meet men who are interested in a committed relationship (read: marriageable). These same institutions, as well as secular sites such as local museums, public libraries, and even certain shopping centers, may also offer broader activities or events that are a good way to expand your horizons — and social network — in general. (An incorrigible beachophile, I'm partial to Santa Monica's free summer concerts on the pier for music and mingling.) So not only will you be delving into something new and hopefully enjoyable, but you also may connect with someone interesting along the way.

If none of the aforementioned suggestions resonate with you, then an outstanding resource for getting involved in new activities (and meeting dating prospects in the process) is Meetup. com. A variety of both mainstream and more esoteric activities are listed—and trying out a few will help determine which ones men gravitate to. For instance, meetups like rollerblading, local happy hour events, and school specific ones such as "Ivy Plus" tend to draw large numbers of men. Although not exclusive to singles, everyone is there with the aim of meeting each other, so conversation is easy. Independently of Meetup, the same goes for the local chapter of your alma mater, ivy covered or not. Coming full circle back to out-of-box strategizing, yet another advantage of Meetup.com is that if there isn't an activity included that interests you, you can always start one.

Finally, besides planning a fortuitous "chance" meeting, it's also advantageous in life to take chances yourself. To illustrate, thirty-two-year-old Madison works as a concierge at a five-star hotel. She had been flirting with a friendly, good-looking guest all week when one morning, out of the blue, he invited her to fly to San Francisco and spend the day with him there. At first she declined his invitation, thinking it was just too ludicrous, and besides, she couldn't abruptly leave work. However, recalling a session with me a few weeks back where we discussed challenging oneself outside of one's comfort zone, she got a coworker to cover for her and went along on the day trip. Fourteen months later their relationship is sheer bliss.

Matchmaker, Matchmaker: The Truth About Setups (Post-College)

Another proactive way to play life's game of chance is to ask friends if they know any unattached men who they think would be right for you. Note that a woman who seeks a serious relationship will markedly increase the odds of finding one this way because when men are willing to be set up, they're typically looking for a girlfriend. Of course less formal group gatherings are always a good way to meet potential dating partners as well, but blind dating becomes increasingly relevant for people of both sexes who are out of school. For instance, UCLA social psychology professor Benjamin Karney, PhD, discusses the "proximity effect," whereby colleges "throw a lot of available partners into a compressed space." He also emphasizes that people often find the person they eventually will marry at college because colleges provide lots of opportunities for intense interaction through class projects, extracurricular activities, and social events.

In addition to Karney's observations, schools enable potential relationships even before you arrive on campus. Specifically, college has already at least generally curated men for you regarding current interests and/or future aspirations; meaning you and the dude down the aisle in Calculus I may already overlap professionally (even if it's only because this course, required for your respective majors, will likely be entirely useless to your eventual jobs). And building on Karney's proximity effect, a woman enrolled in a university or college is exposed to large numbers of guys to date—not just on campus but also through friends—and friends of friends at other schools. Therefore, she has a good chance of finding a boyfriend who, for example, was a friend of her roommate who dated his brother (okay, you get the idea). Additionally, there is already at least one shared commonality between two otherwise arbitrary people: an association with college culture. However, once the campus stomping grounds and collegial network of connections become less readily available (i.e., after graduation) it becomes far more difficult to *spontaneously* meet such large numbers of potential partners. But "more difficult" does not mean impossible. Especially if you're open to being set up.

Although both men and women in high-pressure jobs often enjoy unwinding at the end of a long, busy day in a club or bar, the "hunting" sometimes grows tiresome. And even if you do meet someone you like by going to the "right" places, a random person you meet at a bar is not necessarily going to be in sync timing-wise with what you want out of a relationship. In addition, you two are not necessarily going to share enough of what I refer to as compatible "lifegrounds" (the totality of one's values, goals, ambitions, attitudes, lifestyle, experiences, and cultural choices) to form a connection past an immediate attraction. So this is where blind dating comes in. Any well-intentioned friend or acquaintance will likely have some insight into what you're looking for and set you up with good — no, make that great — matches. Just like the savvy mutual friend who realized she knew someone, in her own words, "perfect" for her longtime guy-pal upset about his dating life and ready to settle down — that setup eventually resulted in a recent royal Brit betrothal with requisite full-on fairy-tale wedding. Bottom line: If a prince of a guy (literally!) and beautiful American actress Meghan Markle each braved blind dating (including with others before they met), then what's stopping *you*?

Cleaning Up Your Hot Mess

A woman who unabashedly admits that her dating life is a helluva hot mess — or nonexistent — should be admired for her straightforward honesty, rather than sanctimoniously judged (typically by those in less-than-perfect relationships themselves). Everyone understands how difficult it is to meet people. *Blind dating (like digital dating) is a fact of our busy existence; there is no more of a stigma to being set up than there is to being a workaholic.*

While other dating rituals such as dance cards and drive-in movies have long since fallen by the wayside, blind dating has managed to survive and thrive over the decades. The reason is simple: it works. Note that Karney's review of over four hundred surveys and studies found that the number-one way that couples met was through friends. Although this finding also includes meeting in very low-pressure group environments (so technically not blind), the sheer volume is nonetheless consistent with my experience. Based on anecdotal observations, I'd say one out of every four couples of all ages that I come in contact with — in and out of my office — reports having met on a blind date

In fact, any couple who has ever met one another through friends, whether or not "blind," has both capitalized on and contributed to a far-reaching sociocultural phenomenon: the wonder of the world's six degrees of separation. So do let trusted friends, family, and colleagues know that you are open to being set up. This is really where you may need to call upon some of that optimism discussed in Step 2 to persist, even after some horrific "WTF were they thinking?!" blind dates. Think of it as a raffle; you're probably not going to draw the winning ticket (or great guy) on the first try. But keep playing and one of those setups is bound to be life changing. The take-home: *take the chance.*

Matchmaking Services Welcome Beautiful Women

An added level of risk comes into play when you take a chance with a pricey matchmaking service, essentially a form of commercial blind dating, because now you've also invested money in addition to time and energy in arranging for an introduction. Matchmaking agencies rely heavily on the skill, often intuitive, of the intermediaries, that is, the matchmakers, who typically handpick matches. The businesses have a vested interest in matching their clients up successfully because happy, amorous power couples will in turn lead to new referrals. However, one downside to the services (besides the often hefty cost) is that women sometimes complain that the men they meet through the agencies seem to be looking for an "11" in terms of looks, yet the women rate themselves as "only" an 8 or 9. I surmise that the relatively large sum of money men spend for an introduction (typically beginning at $5,000) perhaps unrealistically affects their expectations in other ways as well. For instance, according to an inside source: one male patron who paid a whopping thirty-five grand for three months of unlimited dates via a high-end Manhattan agency requested a "model with an Ivy League degree" (yes, really) and then was dissatisfied because his gorgeous date hailed from NYU.

In general, men who use matchmaking services put a premium on women's looks regardless of what other qualities they seek in a mate, analogous to some female patrons who predominantly value men's bank accounts. At any rate, if you're a busy woman with more cash than time and are seeking a man motivated to shell out big bucks to meet his soul mate, then a matchmaking agency may at least be worth a try. However, be sure to vet a few, including talking to current or former female clients, if possible, as well as reading online reviews before handing over money. Better yet, according to the best available research (by a curious single female blogger) if you are "very attractive, fit, book smart and street smart, and have a successful career of some sort," you'll likely get on a high-end matchmaking roster for free. Just make sure you're under forty. Gratefully, that setup (so to speak) is far removed from spontaneous, "real-world" encounters where a woman can be incredibly appealing to the right guy regardless of her age.

Step 4 Playlist ♫
Cabaret/Liza Minnelli
Matchmaker, Matchmaker/Jerry Bock

I hate these blurred lines
I know you want it . . . but you're a good girl

—Robin Thicke, Pharrell Williams

Step 5

Hooking Up: More Than Just Friends

kay, so your secret crush has friend zoned you. Don't lose hope: things can still change. Especially if you understand how. That's where Step 5 comes in to explain an important hidden psychological advantage that most women don't realize they have with men whom they already know, even just in passing. The "familiarity phenomenon," detailed below, is a simple "default" advantage that women don't have to expend any effort to cultivate. But capitalizing on this unique psychological dynamic often takes a woman's relationship with a male friend or acquaintance to a whole new level. In fact, this little-known phenomenon explains precisely how and why you and that crush may actually be predisposed to falling in love. You'll also begin to understand when sex truly isn't casual as much as coercive, and why your instincts almost never steer you wrong. Sober instincts, that is; as will become apparent, the brain's flimsy guardrail between consensual (if regrettable) drunken sex and drunken, *incapacitated* sexual victimization may not prevent a deadly fall.

The Familiarity Phenomenon

Pivotal research by Stanford University social psychologist Robert Zajonc, PhD, has led to the well-established psychosocial "familiarity-likeability" principle. Simply stated, the more familiar a particular face is — that is, the more often we are exposed to the same person — the more likeable he or she becomes to us. This psychological phenomenon also explains, in large measure, why people are so starstruck over celebrities: they already feel they "know" them from seeing their faces so often. It makes all the difference to understand that familiarity doesn't breed contempt, but rather "contentness," or likeability. Keep this in mind when you consider talking to that cute guy you always see at your gym, or that down-the-street neighbor you frequently notice out walking his dog — or even that lawyer-with-the-great-smile who gets off the elevator one floor ahead of you. If you're attracted to a man you keep crossing paths with but have previously felt too shy or awkward to approach, the familiarity principle predicts that he would (at a minimum) be fine with a greeting just from seeing you repeatedly. This is because studies consistently show that people rate "familiar" strangers as more likeable than complete strangers. (My hypothesis for why this happens is that basic survival needs are met while babies are in direct contact with the *familiar* faces of their primary caretakers; hence facial familiarity becomes associated early in life with immensely positive feelings of safety, nurturance, and comfort.) Overcoming your shyness or trepidation to approach a familiar man you wish to know better with a simple hello is empowering in itself and, given the right timing and circumstances, may lead to much more.

Consider the story of an acquaintance of mine. In her forties and divorced, Denise was tired of dead-end dating with a string of damaged men; by her own admission she was ready to give up. In part to release the tension brought on by her dismal dating life, she would regularly swim at a large university pool. Over time she and another regular swimmer there began chatting. But Denise believed that despite being attracted to the blond, muscular fellow aquaphile, she "didn't have a chance" because he was several years her junior. Nevertheless, after about a year of casual poolside conversations, Denise found herself asking him if he'd like to get coffee sometime. So instead of throwing in the towel, Denise continued to swim laps — but now she happily swims alongside her hunky husband. It's doubtful that this couple would have initially even begun dating, however, without the familiarity phenomenon at play.

What Turns a Friend into a Boyfriend? (It's Not What You Think)

The same principle applies with "just friends." Regarding that go-to guy whom you *now* find yourself interested in having a relationship with—somehow let him know. At the very least, the familiarity-likeability principle alone gives you a slight advantage. Furthermore, some of the happiest romantic pairings begin platonically. In support of this fact, a survey sample of 2,037 nationwide married couples by Brigham Young University researchers found that relationships that began with friendship versus hot sex scored higher in happiness, faithfulness, and longevity. Even considering the potential bias in a study affiliated with a religious institution that prohibits premarital sex among students, its implications are nonetheless significant. Although I usually don't begin cocktail party conversations by asking random spouses about their sex lives, some of the happiest couples of all ages I've known over the years began their relationships as friends. (And incidentally, I do tend to ask couples how they met.)

The problem is that often people believe that they'll somehow irrevocably damage the friendship if they assert their wishes for more. This is where subtlety and tact come into play: you can allude to how you feel over time without spilling out something akin to "true confessions." For instance, let loose an occasional line like, "It's weird, I had a dream that you and I were together." Then notice how your friend responds; if he outwardly rejects or persistently ignores or acts oblivious to these hints or more overt communications, back off. In contrast, a male friend who secretly harbors romantic feelings toward you will jump at the chance to take things further. In fact, he's already probably tormented by having you only in the friend zone and merely *imagining* what you look like naked. But don't make the mistake of believing that sleeping with your male BFF will automatically turn him into your soul mate. Note that "I care a lot about you" is not the same as "I'm in love with you." In fact, without at least a semblance of mutual romantic love to accompany the sex and propel the friendship to another level, you'll either become "friends with benefits," or newly awkward friends.

Or worse.

One of my patients, Jessica, described how she had been best friends and close confidantes with a fellow classmate all through law school until the weekend they graduated—and slept together. Not having heard from her friend for several days afterward, Jessica finally "blinked first" and texted him. Since then, most of their communications have primarily focused on how they both realize "it" was a mistake; "it" wouldn't have happened had they both not been "entirely wasted" and so on. Then there's Brittany who slept with her male BFF David "just once," and apparently the sex was wonderful, no regrets. However, heretofore each other's wingman at parties and bars, Brittany now finds herself annoyed when David flirts with other women in her presence. Also, she no longer tolerates listening to him discuss new women in his life at length. While both Jessica and Brittany remain friends with their best buds, ironically the closeness doesn't feel as cozy as before.

Still, given the familiarity-likeability principle, if both of you are *mutually* romantically attracted to one another and the timing is right, the odds of your longstanding buddy becoming a seriously significant boyfriend are in your favor. On a sweet, if sentimental, reflective note, even the most resolute (fictional) bachelor in musical theatre, Henry Higgins of *My Fair Lady*, softened toward a potential love interest only at the very moment he realized, "I've grown accustomed to her face."

"Can You Imagine Us Years from Today . . . ?"

Does romance stand a chance even after the passage of decades in cases where former friends may not even have been in contact with one another? A resounding yes: it's very common for old high school friends or acquaintances to take up where they left off. Remarkably, psychology professor Nancy Kalish, PhD, discovered in her "Lost Loves" project—a study of 1,001 people aged eighteen to eighty-nine who tried reunions with former sweethearts—that old flames burn the hottest. According to Kalish, "People who later rekindle romances with lost loves often experience the most intense emotional satisfaction of their lives." Notably, the "stay together" rate for first loves (high school/college sweethearts, etc.) reunited later in life ranges from 72 percent to 78 percent, compared to approximately 66 percent for other serious couplings. Perhaps the familiarity factor overrides time in attracting former classmates to one another, while a mutually recognizable past seals the deal.

Additionally, the study of perception has demonstrated that people often "see" one another as they appeared when they first met. This interesting cognitive quirk, which is not the same as the familiarity phenomenon, undoubtedly fosters romantic feelings between long-term partners and perhaps also contributes to the tendency for former mates to reacquaint—and oftentimes more. To borrow from Simon and Garfunkel's melancholic refrain, "sharing a park bench at seventy" may well become your reality.

The Shadow of Your Smile

But what do you do if a guy whom you've never seen before catches your eye, and you're not likely to run into him ever again? Smile at him and start some small talk. In my experience as a psychologist, I've discovered men are actually more afraid of initial rejection than women are. I constantly hear laments from men about how they found themselves right next to an attractive woman at a grocery store, or even in an elevator, where they had an opportunity to speak to her and then later regret that they didn't! So you start talking first. Whether or not the conversation leads anywhere (such as an exchange of contact information), it is still great practice in flirty chitchat—so an altogether "win-win" situation.

It doesn't even matter if your small talk is — in my patients' words — hopelessly lame; it's your smile that actually speaks volumes. A study conducted at the University of British Columbia last year demonstrated that men prefer women with a smile on their faces because they are most sexually attracted to women who look happy. This preference seems to be hardwired into men's brains early on, as evidenced by a 2007 research study published in the *European Journal of Developmental Psychology*. The study demonstrated that even infants stare the longest at smiling faces. And incidentally, if a guy you're dating is responsible for your (big) smile, be sure and let him know: I've heard from a number of men (ranging from a twenty-three-year-old professional basketball player to a fiftysomething-year-old plastic surgeon) that they tend to fall for women whom they know they're making happy.

To illustrate how truly powerful a smile can be, consider the fact that the model for Leonardo da Vinci's well-known masterpiece wasn't considered a great beauty in her day. In fact, she was a very ordinary-looking married woman who commissioned the painting to commemorate the birth of her second son. Nevertheless, her alluring, timeless smile made that painting arguably the most famous in history, bestowing goddess-like status on its subject, Lisa Gherardini, otherwise known as Mona Lisa.

Hookups That Unhinge

Once my lover now my friend, what a cruel thing to pretend
–Fiona Apple

Even when your sexy gaze meets its mark, there's a huge chasm between merely smiling at a guy and hooking up with him. Here the term "hooking up" is used to denote having casual sex, whether oral sex, intercourse, or other intense sexual activity. (So French kissing makes the cut, but if he plants a kiss on your closed lips you haven't hooked up — although he certainly wants to.) According to nationwide college-aged survey participants, the context or setting is typically less formal than a date. Additionally, there is not the expectation of a relationship, nor is one precluded.

Of course, one could argue that the phrase "casual sex" is in itself an oxymoron for women. As author Wendy Shalit points out in *A Return to Modesty: The Lost Virtue,* women have been known to be "less enthusiastic" about these hookups than men. Shalit's claim was first supported by health and sex educator Roberta Ogletree, PhD, when her 1993 study of college women's sexual behavior found that approximately 70 percent of 656 college women surveyed reported they had been "verbally coerced" into having "unwanted sex." Based on my discussions with women, this hasn't changed much today, whether applied to casual hookups or more structured dates. Such coercion is actually emotional blackmail that may involve guilt-tripping, obligation, and often anger or fake "hurt" on the part of the guy.

Consider a twenty-two-year-old patient's recent experience. Nina, a dog walker, was excited about an upcoming first date to a romantic rooftop restaurant with a "Ferrari-driving" Pomeranian puppy owner she really liked (or thought she did). By our next session, however, Nina was in tears regretting that after dinner, upon going to his house to "visit Lucky," she let Pom-guy persuade her to "take off my top and give [him] head when we hadn't even kissed yet." She further explained that when she tried to back out, he sneered, "That's not how I roll." Although technically not considered sexual assault, coercive or "railroaded" sex still makes women feel manipulated, used, and/or resentful during and after these encounters — encounters where social conformity and male power plays run amok.

Similarly, Donna Freitas, author of *The End of Sex: How Hookup Culture Is Leaving a Generation Unhappy, Sexually Unfulfilled, and Confused about Intimacy,* surveyed 1,230 college students across the country in 2006. She found that of students who reported hooking up, 41 percent used words such as "regretful," "empty," "miserable," "disgusted," "ashamed," "duped," and even "abused" to describe the experience. Even more telling, Freitas noted that during one-on-one interviews, the students said that even if they didn't like hooking up, "they [pretended] they [did] because it's such a big part of campus social life." Confirming these accounts, I've similarly observed through both my practice as well as participation on college panels that this stance also applies to male students, who mostly don't really enjoy begrudging, uninspired sex. Or, what so many women relate to as "icky," unpleasant, or just plain awful. As Freitas puts it, "Nervous to be alone in challenging hookup culture, most students go along with it, even if they privately long for alternatives." There's that pesky problem of conformity again. For both sexes.

Still, that gut-wrenching, post-sex emotional black hole is categorically owned by women. Heretofore silenced, vulnerable voices are echoed in the poignant words of many of the college women who submitted their stories to aforementioned *New York Times* journalists Bennett and Jones. For instance, Sarah of South Carolina recounts a sexual partner "sharply" responding to her morning-after "shaken" quest for clarity with, "I didn't do anything you didn't want." She continues: "It's been months since, and I'm still left with a dread and an underlying guilt that reaching this point of violation and confusion was somehow my fault." And Livia recalls her "younger me" as "entering the dating and hookup scene with low self-esteem and little knowledge." She explains her then-inability to refuse performing oral sex as feeling "contractually obligated to take the guy to the end and expect nothing in return."

Or, as Freitas reflects, "The guiding commandment of hookup culture: Thou shalt not become attached to your partner." Shalit takes this cynical stance even further when she laments, "It is okay to treat women like prostitutes, because nobody cares." While this may be a bit harsh, Shalit's insights are particularly prescient. Notably, at one Catholic college Freitas investigated, an all-girls first-year hall was dubbed "Virgin Vault" at the beginning of the year by senior men at the college. By the end of the year they called it the "Slut Hut." Similarly, I've known upperclassmen to brand incoming female freshmen as "piglets"; perhaps those guys are actually self-identifying as, well, pigs. Macho bravado aside, women should realize that for some men at least, unhinging themselves from an objectified woman whom they casually sleep with — and "humorously" demean — is just as easy as hooking up with her in the first place.

Not to mention self-serving.

Interestingly, the term "hookup" originated in Nena and George O'Neill's 1972 book *Open Marriage* to justify, well, open marriage. The O'Neills, who were married, speciously argued that spouses should have sex outside their marriage to fulfill potentially unrealized, unique "hook-up points." Here's how they put it: "Imagine each person as an organism covered with thousands of antennae. Each of these facets, or antennae is a hook-up point that makes it possible for us to reach out and connect with other human beings. . . . What then happens to your hook-up points your mate then cannot match? . . . They become so deadened they will simply drop off, making you a diminished person with fewer points of contact." In other words, go and screw someone (or many) other than your spouse so your "hook-up points" don't fall off, rendering you inferior somehow.

The O'Neills also admonish, "The man you marry today, sad to say, may not be the father of your child tomorrow. Nor will your wife necessarily be the mother of your children. She may be, but don't count on it." Great, so instead of fulfilling romantic yearnings, the essence of hookups harks back to marital infidelity, including indifference to whom you get pregnant by! *End of Modesty* author Wendy Shalit nails it, "Our sexual language is already soaked in the landscape of betrayal before we've even begun."

I'd guess the women in the "Slut Hut," who were likely swept away by the heady, newfound freedom of college life and overwhelmed by men's advances, might feel betrayed by that label. At the very least they wouldn't be flattered. Nor should they be. The Online College Social Life Survey, which surveyed twenty-four thousand students at twenty-one universities between 2005 and 2011, found a lingering sexual double standard. That's where males who "score" frequent sexual encounters are typically admired by other males, while women who do the same are derogated or stigmatized — to say the least. According to the study's author, New York University sociologist Paula England, PhD, this double standard causes men to "disrespect" the very women who hook up with them. It is this same double standard that is responsible for the highly damaging, judgmental term "slut shaming" applied to anything from a woman's clothing to her sexual activity. Dr. England was being tactful, if not downright understating the problem, in her choice of the word "disrespect."

Outrageously insulting is more like it.

For instance, I've counseled a few women who related how they decided to explore their sexuality in college by sleeping with various different guys. (One even was dead set on losing her virginity this way.) Although for these women it really was just about sex — not about desiring a relationship — they were rightfully surprised, hurt, and oftentimes outright humiliated for weeks afterward when the men would pointedly ignore them in class or avoid them in common areas like the library or cafeteria. As USC sophomore Kayla bluntly put it, "I'm fine to finger fuck, but not good enough to sit next to."

Not surprisingly, nationwide surveys show most sexual assaults on campus happen during the first two years at school, exactly when the Catholic school upperclassmen were "playfully" disparaging freshman females and my patients were being shunned by their hookup partners. Even assuming that the sex was completely consensual, and the college men's reference to "sluts" was rendered in jest, I've heard many men refer to women they've hooked up with (but never their girlfriends) by the only slightly less offensive, but equally derogatory, term "promiscuous." (Substitute "ho" or "skanky" here if the guy is under thirty.) The name-calling appears to be especially pronounced when the woman's hookup partners share a common network such as teammates, fraternity brothers, or (clubby) professional colleagues. Speaking of "bro culture," in a far different scenario where your serious-ish boyfriend is more into bromance than romance, it still might be wise to think twice before you hook up with his best buddy, regardless of how rocky your relationship may be. Your guy will never forget it — nor will he let you forget it either. At any rate, whether you choose to have sex solely for pleasure, excitement, experimentation, adventure, awakening, physical affirmation, human connection, in-the-moment intimacy, loneliness salve, or (hopefully not) revenge, at least be aware that however egregiously offensive, double-standard shaming still exists. And consider this: multitudinous, consecutive casual hookups (for both genders) are like the Russian roulette of sexual partners—eventually you get the one from hell.

Your Guardian Angel: Instincts

Even if you're dead set on hooking up, especially with multiple partners, it helps to listen to your instincts to avoid potentially dangerous situations. This holds just as true with long-term friends as it does when you've just barely met someone.

Interestingly, I've noticed that unlike men who tend to trust their instincts, women often will (detrimentally) talk themselves out of their own gut intuition. One possible explanation for this difference is that portions of the brain's limbic system, or "emotional brain" structures involved in reading emotions and emotional decision making, have less densely packed neural substrates in males than females. This means that men operate in much more of a "black-and-white" way than do women, who tend to infuse their emotional decisions with nuance and seemingly endless analysis. This also accounts in part for why men have an easier time leaving a partner who has cheated on them than women. And why women get so frustrated when their guy walks out of the room in the heat of an argument. Our brains want to talk it out; theirs don't.

Note that the root of the word intuition (*tuere*) is Latin for "to protect." In *The Gift of Fear*, violence expert Gavin de Becker contends that you know when you are in danger because, "You have the gift of a brilliant internal guardian that stands ready to warn you of hazards and guide you through risky situations." Psychologically, the reason intuition is so powerful is precisely because emotion and reason seamlessly work together for the sole purpose of protecting you.

Drunken Sex — Regret or Worse?

While your "internal guardian" or intuition will keep you from harm's way, if it is silenced, then it can't do its job. Neurologically, instincts simultaneously draw on judgment and reasoning as well as emotion and memory; in other words, highly efficient brain functioning. However, if your thought process is suppressed or altogether shut off by the effects of drugs or alcohol, then your instincts can't protect you. Specifically, when you're drinking too much it's harder to think clearly or sense a dangerous situation. Don't become a statistic: a Justice Department survey of 6,800 female undergraduates at the University of Wisconsin and University of Montana claimed that nearly 14 percent reported having been the victim of at least one sexual assault at college. More than half the victims said they were incapacitated from drugs or alcohol at the time. Bottom line: know your limits as to how much you can drink, especially, and still remain fully in control of your decisions and actions so that nobody can take advantage of an altered state of consciousness.

And if you don't know your limits, don't test them. In other words, don't become so drunk or high that your reactions are unduly compromised, making you a target for unwanted sexual contact. (Some college men discuss actually "targeting" specific women for sex, for instance during an upcoming party.) However, even that may just be the tip of the iceberg. In *The Hunting Ground,* a 2015 documentary about campus sexual assault, one male student explains how he preys on inebriated women he can "overpower"; his admitted MO is to offer to "help" a girl outside for air or upstairs to "sleep it off" — and then assault her. Neurologically our wiring presents a slippery slope; it's only a quick slide (especially if you're pushed) from drunken sex, where your poor judgment leads to next-day regret, and being so wasted that you can't consent at all. Alcohol and drugs set up the perfect storm for sexual assault: they incapacitate women and embolden certain men to forgo what little conscience or moral margins may have been there in the first place. Especially with impaired impulse control thrown into the mix. And even when the woman is sober, alcohol gives guys with an agenda warped confidence and "courage" to tune out your protests. These same guys are equally tone-deaf to your "not-into-it" bodily cues. So despite all your negative verbalizations and no-go body language, he keeps pressuring. (Note to men: coercion is not seduction, and sleazy is not sexy.)

Women attending the same college or even in the same general social network as men they party with tend to be especially trusting. While you don't have to be paranoid (defined as *unreasonably* fearful), it's especially important nonetheless to remain cautiously aware. This applies even in situations where you yourself are not drinking much but others are. There's the added benefit in such a scenario of being able to help a friend who may be in trouble.

It's also not paranoid these days to watch your drink—as in, don't let it out of your sight. Take it with you even when you go to the bathroom. And regardless of who offers to get you a glass of champagne at a bar or party, go with him and watch it being poured. Fast-acting drugs can be slipped into drinks undetected by even faster acting fingers. Plus, as pathetically preposterous as it seems, a guy you know — or think you know — might be the one who messes with your martini.

The "New" Rape Culture on Campus

Stranger-predator rape is actually the least of college women's worries; among the approximately nine hundred Justice Department college survey participants who had reported being sexually assaulted, the vast majority of assaults were by someone the women knew. Similarly, my review of sexual assault data at a small liberal arts college in southern California where I've been involved with sexual assault assessment and prevention corroborates the fact that of the approximately thirty-two assaults reported in one year serious enough to warrant investigation, the student almost always knew her assailant.

What some men have trouble grasping is that just because hookup culture is acceptable, that doesn't mean it's okay for them to push for a hookup with their study buddy/dorm mate/lab partner. So when he tries to kiss you, he'll probably respect a face-saving (his), lightly worded "C'mon, cut it out" or a stronger "Hey, don't!" and stop. Unless, once again, he (or you) are drinking to excess, when all too often, put simply, he won't.

The problem is that some men use their own fallacious "logic" (convincing themselves that a false notion is true) to assume that if a girl is drinking a lot, she's down for casual sex. Especially with him. Especially because you and he may have shared a laugh or two in the past, or even that evening. No, this reasoning makes no sense whatsoever, but try telling that to a horny, drunk dude who is dead set on hooking up with you. And although you're definitely an easier mark when you drink, even your Diet Coke won't deter the wrong person. What these guys are missing (besides a moral compass), is that just because hookup culture normalizes *consensual* casual sex, it doesn't normalize casual sex between friends/acquaintances/dating partners where the woman doesn't (or can't) green light intimate physical contact. Actually, that's called assault.

The entertainment industry, in particular, has recently been called to task for its "open secret" complicity in anything from sexual harassment to assault and worse. But as the #MeToo movement has highlighted, women in nearly every workplace and reach of community life, from those who scrub floors to those who are given the floor, have all too often been considered fair game for sexual sport by someone in a position of power over them. And among college classmates, a power differential isn't even necessary for women's degradation.

In fact, rape culture is commonly defined as a culture in which violence and sexual assaults against women are common, and in which attitudes like victim blaming, sexism, machoism, and media objectification of women are used to excuse, tolerate, and sometimes even condone rape. My insider lens into the "he said; she said" of sexual assault arbitration on college campuses is that the prevalence of consensual hookups along with drinking has given (some) men one more "excuse" to justify their assaultive behavior and often incredibly deny having committed a rape. Even sadder, they occasionally truly believe their own lies.

The last time I checked, drinking wasn't a crime. (And, yes, that "Thirsty Thursday" rum punch may indeed momentarily help you escape the week's crazy pressures.) But given the reality of the "new" rape culture, it doesn't hurt to be preemptively smart and aware. Face down rather than fall down that alcohol-reeking rabbit hole; all it takes is another beer or shot or two to turn a feel-good buzz into a worst-night nightmare.

Relationship Smarts — or Relationship Suicide

Relationship Smarts	**Relationship Suicide**
Guy BFF becomes soul mate	Sleep with a guy BFF pre-romance
Seriously selective sex	Sleep with guys in same fraternity, team, etc.
Talk things out with boyfriend	Hook up with his best friend
Be sure	Hook up out of obligation versus desire
Dump deadbeat dude	Ignore your instincts
Nice, manageable buzz okay	So drunk or high your judgment is jeopardized
Sports Illustrated-ish sexts	Send pics of yourself topless or naked

---

Step 5 Playlist ♫
Blurred Lines/Robin Thicke, Pharrell Williams
Old Friends/Simon and Garfunkel
The Shadow of Your Smile/Tony Bennett
Shadowboxer/Fiona Apple

I go online, and my breath catches in my chest until I hear three little words: you've got mail. I hear nothing. Not even a sound on the streets of New York, just the beating of my own heart. I have mail. From you.

—Kathleen Kelly, *You've Got Mail*

Step 6

Do Online Smart: Myths and Musts

*R*ob was a divorced, forty-nine-year-old exotic car enthusiast, a perfect-on-paper stockbroker whom Ashley couldn't wait to meet—until he proudly texted his "junk" to her. (And I don't mean bonds!) And let's not forget Andrew, the charming fifty-two-year-old anesthesiologist who insisted on a high-end, pricey restaurant for his first date with Lauren; after ordering a much more expensive meal than she did, he also insisted on splitting the bill. Or take Mark, the adorably funny twenty-six-year-old veterinary assistant who showed great promise in his thoughtful, witty notes to Sydney, until he ducked out midway through their first date claiming a dog in his care was "having a panic attack." She almost believed him, until she never heard from him again. But none of these top Rebecca's "ringer": excited to finally meet Todd after several engaging phone conversations, Rebecca spied him removing a wedding ring just as she was walking into the romantic French bistro he'd chosen for their first rendezvous.

Welcome to the world of online dating.

That is a new welcome unless you're already one of the approximately 38 million Americans, or 15 percent of the adult population, who have used an online dating site or mobile dating app (according to a 2015 Pew survey). And if you're in a fairly new committed relationship, there's a very good chance it began online: among Americans who've been with their spouse or partner five years or less, 12 percent met on a dating site or app. What's more, independent surveys show the average time from meeting to marriage is just under eighteen months for couples who met online, versus 3.5 years for offline couples, which suggests a high degree of motivation to meet a spouse among the online daters. Those numbers corroborate the findings of psychology professor Eli Finkel, PhD, who led a team that reviewed over four hundred psychology studies and public interest surveys on how couples meet. The extensive study found digital dating to be the second most common way couples now get together, surpassed only by meeting through friends. These staggering statistics together suggest that if your physical surroundings aren't exactly teeming with single men, it may behoove you to become better — if not braver — at online dating.

Incidentally, former patients Ashley and Rebecca eventually met their husbands through Internet dating sites (OkCupid and JDate, respectively); Sydney and Lauren are currently in long-term relationships with men they likewise met online (Match). However, all four women persevered through periodic bouts of seriously deflated self-esteem and crippling disillusionment with digital matchmaking. It took a bit of strategizing and a lot of handholding (mine, not their dates') to keep the women from giving up. Fortunately they didn't!

Persistence Pays Off (So Does Living in Seattle)

A good rule of thumb is to treat online dating as a diet staple, meaning it's always there if you choose to partake, but it can't be your sole source of relationship sustenance. When you find yourself unduly frustrated in your online search, it's best to take a break. That said, persistence pays off. Specifically, a team headed by computational sociologist Elizabeth Bruch, PhD, studied 187,000 internet dating users (of a free, unnamed site) across four US cities — New York, Chicago, Boston and Seattle — using PageRank algorithm, which is also used by Google to rank website search engine results. The month-long study, published in the August, 2018 issue of *Science Advances*, found men's reply rate to the "average" message to be between zero and ten percent. Given these low rates, common sense dictates that the more persistent (and perhaps thick-skinned) you are at investing time and energy to write messages, the more responses you'll eventually garner.

Conversely, regarding your own replies to men's openers, try responding to at least a few more guys who send you enthusiastic, positively worded messages. Unexpectedly, Bruch found men had slightly *lower* reply rates from women to whom they initially wrote longer, more positive messages. Equally surprising, men sent such wordier opening messages to women deemed less "desirable" by the algorithm; with desirability ranked by how many first messages users received, in conjunction with whether the senders themselves were receiving initial messages. So it could be the men wrote longer openings to nonetheless appealing women they assumed were less likely to reject them relative to highly desirable, out-of-their-league women, with whom they instead played it "cool." Interestingly, Seattle was the only city where men *consistently* sent women — desirable or not — the longest initial messages. (Perhaps that's because, according to the researchers, Seattle's ratio of men to women is two to one for much of the user population — suggesting that Seattle men have to try harder to attract a date.) Regardless of where you live, study results (especially women's low reply rates to clearly interested men) support my contention that if you stop looking so hard for a "perfect" partner, but instead keep an eye out for hints of a kindred, kind spirit, you could very well find a real, multidimensional man who turns out to be *deeply* desirable — and dedicated — to you.

How to Stand Out

So how do you attract a man online you actually want to meet? (Short of moving to Seattle.) You've got to do *you*, but do it with clever, original descriptors. For example, the descriptor "slender" only gives half the picture. However, slender together with "I really rock my jeans" will help you stand out from the rest of the skinnies. Similarly, note the difference between "I like trying new restaurants" and "I'm an incurable foodie." In other words, use language effectively to give catchy, colorful examples of generic traits.

Additionally, if there is an author or artist you love, say so. There may just be a fellow John Grisham, Kurt Vonnegut, or Stieg Larsson reader out there whose eye you'll catch. In fact, a few men have told me that the affinity for a common author or book was what attracted them to a particular woman online. And opposites sometimes really do attract as well. To illustrate, one of my patients met her future husband, an admittedly hopeless Trekkie (avid fan of Star Trek), through a dating site where she'd mentioned that she hated science fiction. As her husband jokingly related, he chose to date her because he didn't want to be with someone who was "nerdish" like himself!

It's also helpful to toss something funny into your profile. (That's also a good way to rule out dudes with no sense of humor.) For instance, instead of just saying that she's a "homebody," I advised one woman to write, "I need someone to sit and watch *Homeland* with me on Sunday nights—while he massages my feet." If you're lacking in creativity, ask a friend with solid writing skills and an even more solid funny bone to help.

There are also situations where you may need to distinguish yourself to rule out the wrong men as much as to reel in the right ones. Consider Charlotte's problem. A Cameron Diaz look-alike with striking profile pictures, Charlotte, a busy executive, has been wasting precious time and energy going out with numerous men she meets online who appear on the up and up—at first. But after a few dates it's clear that these tools are primarily interested in sex. I recently advised Charlotte to add the following "screening" sentence to her profile: "I'm interested in an eventual relationship; if you're not, then don't even bother." As of this writing we don't know how that's going to fly, but I'm betting on Charlotte baiting better guys.

Keep It Real

A seventeen-year-old patient of mine, Kalib, recently requested that I review an essay he wrote for a college admission application. The college asked him to pretend he was writing a note to a future roommate that "reveals something that will help your roommate — and us — know you better." It occurred to me that the admission question hoped to draw honest, revelatory responses that would uncover an applicant's true essence in much the same way that the best profiles do. For example, saying that you like to travel really says nothing about yourself because so does almost everyone else. Such "self-disclosure" is analogous to the student who says he "works hard" and "enjoys spending time with friends." Once again, these attributes could be applied to nearly anyone.

Like the college applicant, take time to think of something that sets you apart from the rest of the pack, no matter how seemingly trivial. You'll draw much better matches that way. For instance, a woman who writes that she "likes to eat the tops of muffins" (à la *Seinfeld*'s Elaine) may come off as neurotic to some men with whom she would probably not be compatible anyway. But those who are attracted to this statement would undoubtedly "get" her cute quirkiness. Similarly, the simple statement, "I am a third-generation preppy rebel" is at once candid and creative. At the very least, such a description would appeal to someone who could relate or who might be intrigued enough to want to meet you. In other words, keep it real. True self-reflection, resulting in "different" vivid statements like these, also would safeguard against what Professor Harry Reiss of the University of Rochester refers to as "a judgmental 'shopping' mentality that can lead people to objectify their potential partners." (Meaning you're the human version of a shirt a dude casually buys online knowing full well he can easily discard it — and go back online, where there are limitless possibilities, to shop for another. Unless it's a *one-of-a kind* shirt.) Men and women alike really are more drawn to unique people whose profiles "click" with them versus clone-like versions of everyone else. And in an increasingly digitized world offering up a revolving door of dates, conveying a sense of individuality may be more important than ever.

Brainy Is Sexy

If you've got it, flaunt it, and here I don't mean your body, although that works, too, but your brains. So do mention that astrophysics advanced degree you're pursuing or the prize you won in college for coding. I had one patient, Yael, who was a Harvard alumna, yet she didn't mention that in her profile because she (correctly) thought it would intimidate men.

But that also worked in her favor.

Notably, although Yael got fewer responses when she mentioned her highbrow alma mater, the men who did contact her were much better matches. Which meant Yael didn't have to waste time sorting through messages from men with whom she likely wouldn't be compatible anyway. Considering the two great JDate guys whom Yael is currently dating, it's reassuring that our brains may (slowly but surely) be catching up to our beauty in the dating game's unspoken barter system.

Age: It's All About That Vibe

When it comes to your profile, remember: a little bit of fudging is fine, but deception will get you dumped.

It's okay to subtract a year or two; in fact, that will often work in your favor. For example, if you're a young-looking forty-eight, you won't miss out on the guy who arbitrarily decides he doesn't want to date women who are older than forty-five. If the two of you do hit it off, odds are he won't care when he finds out your true age by glancing at your passport while en route to Cabo for a romantic getaway. Remarkably, one Internet dating coach told a woman to say she was ten years younger, and then immediately add that she was "actually slightly older but has a young vibe." Generally, if you lie by over five years or so it's best to set him straight early on. If not, don't be surprised if your guy flees when he learns the truth, no matter how well things seem to have been going.

Your Best Shot: The Dos and Don'ts of Photos

Despite digital dating's emerging emphasis on "substance over selfies" in promoting genuine connections versus superficial hookups, those selfies are still going to be critical in getting you noticed, even by relationship-seeking guys. So please make sure yours work for you. One of my male patients (who is so not-superficial) recently reported that he barely even reads profiles anymore because he can tell much more about a woman's personality from her photos. Even the way the photograph is taken can pack some punch. For instance, a 2010 study of seven thousand profile pictures from OkCupid.com (by its founder who happens to be a Harvard-educated statistician) revealed that men are significantly more likely to respond to pictures of women who look straight at the camera with a pouty smile. In fact, photographs of women who looked up at a phone camera with a coy-flirty face got by far the most messages. Moreover, contrary to what most dating sites tell you, the so-called lower-quality phone or webcam photos were even more successful at getting "flirts" and messages than those taken by higher-end means. Along the same lines, men tend to dismiss contrived-looking portrait studio photographs as deceptive or "artificial." (Unless you're a toddler or kid, I agree.)

And ladies, now isn't the time to shy away from exposing just a bit of boob. In the OkCupid study, women who showed even just a little cleavage got 49 percent more responses than the average photo. The results were even more dramatic with age, so that a thirty-two-year-old showing cleavage received only one fewer contact than her eighteen-year-old online mini-me. Which makes sense considering that the most popular person in Bruch's aforementioned study of 187,000 dating site users was a thirty-year-old woman in New York who received 1,504 messages—equivalent to one message every thirty minutes, round the clock for the entire month! (Although the study didn't include her picture or note her clothing, I'd wager that there was some serious cleavage going on.) Returning to the OkCupid study, it's noteworthy that equally attractive thirtysomething-year-old women who showcased no anatomical assets got on average four fewer messages than did younger women. Blame it on his brain: men make initial psychosexual decisions visually. And note that twisted and/or misogynistic guys are going to send grossly inappropriate messages even if you're dressed like a nun.

Regardless of camera angle, the OkCupid study findings corroborate my own hypothesis that older women generally err in not emphasizing their bodies. The lead researcher underscores the point, however, that in order for messages to lead to meaningful conversation (versus "Hey, nice tits"), then a woman should be doing something interesting in the photo, for example playing a sport. Unique settings/backdrops and travel shots also work well. However, a photograph with your breasts porn-like front and center shout out that's all you have to offer. (I had one patient who drunk-posted a picture of herself braless in a crop top exposing neathage—for the unenlightened, that's the underside of breasts—and then complained about all the "rude" messages from horny guys.) Even when a picture is understatedly sexy, be prepared to rule out the guy with no filter who writes that he "loves your perky boobs." (Dude, *no*.) Subtlety is key all around; at any rate, do lose the snow sweater for your photos.

Speaking of snow, unless you're Olympic skier Lindsey Vonn (or anyone else who has ever graced the cover of *Sports Illustrated*, for that matter), regardless of how cool the goggles look, forget about using them in a primary photo—you know, the one you took skiing last winter where you look like a faceless polar bear. And I emphasize polar bear, not faceless. Regarding faces, here's another fact that may come as a surprise: contrary to most dating sites' instructions, analysis of seven thousand OkCupid.com profile pictures revealed that, all else being equal, showing one's face had no impact on the number of messages a woman received. A faceless image was even advantageous if the photo's subject was "unusual, mysterious, sexy" or otherwise alluring. In other words, the faceless photograph led to an abundance of opening messages if it piqued men's curiosity or interest. Of course, including a great bod with a nondiscernable face never hurts.

And once again, in direct contrast to widely disseminated advice about online profile pictures, men say that they're okay with you using a snapshot that was taken a year or two ago if it bears at least a reasonable facsimile of what you look like now. But please don't use a picture taken of yourself seven years ago when you were ten pounds slimmer; you'll just be setting yourself up for a series of rejections. This may seem like common sense, but you'd be surprised at the number of women I counsel who post pictures that look nothing like their current selves and then can't understand why the guy never calls after they meet.

Finally, and this is very important: men don't want to see another picture of you with your cat. Dogs are fine, however. Just trust me on this one.

Hot Shots: What to Reveal in a Profile Pic (Yes and No)

Yes	No
Hint of cleavage	Breasts front and center
You on the beach	Anything under bikini lines
Faceless photo okay if mysterious/alluring	Hidden face/shapeless body
Emphasize great body at any age	Great body ten years and/or pounds ago
Interesting activity/background	Contrived pose
Dogs or any other animals except cats	You and your cat

Love at First Swipe: Best Dating Apps

Even George Orwell couldn't have imagined that people's future phones would be smart enough to hook them up—and not just for talking. Enter techy Cupid: smartphone apps that connect potential dating partners. But while smartphones may make handy, portable matchmakers, how "smart" they truly are at setting people up mostly depends on who else happens to be using the same app at any given time. Even so, various apps can still be loosely classified based on the "type" of guy who uses each.

The original dating app, Tinder, continues to be the most widely used. As for all those popular Tinder copycat apps with a twist—including Hinge, Bumble, Coffee Meets Bagel, and JSwipe—the latter two are especially favored by my female patients. (I'll describe these five apps in more detail in the coming pages.) The newest app of the bunch, Bumble, is also picking up momentum, but so far reactions from women have been mixed.

Tinder

As philosopher Arthur Schopenhauer put it, "Talent hits the target no one else can hit; genius hits the target no one else can see." That's why Tinder, a 2012 app that convinced popular, attractive college students they needed online dating was nothing short of genius. Online dating was already mainstream at the time, but primarily among older people seeking serious relationships. To note, in 2012 the eHarmony user's average age was forty-two, and a complex compatibility questionnaire was and continues to be required to register. Tinder, in contrast, matches people with one another based mostly on a few Facebook profile pictures they select, as well as on age and current location. (Yes, to use Tinder one must link it to a Facebook account.) Pictures actually serve as the "tinder" that ignites a romantic spark. The real clincher, however, is that only if two people both "like" each other are they allowed to correspond, a radical departure from traditional online dating sites where anyone can message anyone else. Taking the "like" feature even further, users additionally have a limited number of "Super Likes" to convey a higher level of interest in someone. (At the very least, being Super Liked should prevent accidentally overlooking the profile of a guy who is very into you — and vice versa.)

Since it was first founded by childhood friends Sean Rad and Jonathan Badeen, among others, when they attended USC together (debuting at where else but a frat party), Tinder took off full force, boasting over one million matches in its first two months. Originally baiting college men with photos of USC Greek goddess-girls, Tinder effectively revolutionized dating for a whole new generation of singles, particularly those in their twenties and, to a lesser extent, early thirties. The popularity is partly because men and women alike experience a mini-high knowing that someone they think is cute likes them back.

However, that ego boost is sometimes all there is. To note, many men keep swiping without any intention of ever initiating contact, stockpiling matches much as they used to collect baseball cards. And even when the app is used as intended, far too many women have related how upon actually meeting, several guys who swiped right weren't at all the "right" guys for them. To put it bluntly, their matches turned out to be people that they would never want to see again let alone see naked. Then there's all those Tinder guys who make it clear *in person* they just want sex. And that doesn't even include "straight-up" guys who text early on, "Hey gorgeous, you wanna have some fun?" or "I bet you look great with your clothes off." For these reasons thin-skinned women without the ability to laugh at the process may do best to keep away, especially from the men who've become addicted to the app. As Cornell University sophomore Rachel Ellicott observed in *The Huffington Post*, "People don't think of [Tinder] as online dating; they think of it as a game." That may not be much of a stretch considering that Tinder originally asked users whether they wished to message their matches — or *keep playing*.

Hinge

One advantage of Hinge over Tinder is that it only matches people who actually share Facebook friends. The app also provides the full name and contact information of proposed matches, rendering a significant level of accountability over Tinder's potentially disconcerting anonymity. According to founder Justin McLeod, in addition to shared friends, where you went to school and where you now work are also taken into important consideration in Hinge's unique algorithm.

Despite such a data-driven interface, McLeod attributes the app's best connections not to a computer-based algorithm, but to a user's "authenticity," which he defines as "the way a person fills out a profile and engages with people." That's also the reasoning behind Hinge's 2016 relaunch as "the relationship app." In keeping with that moniker, Hinge has replaced swiping with a feature that allows users to comment on photos and profiles. This may be particularly helpful to women in ascertaining who cares enough (and is smart enough) to think about and respond to a prompt they answered.

Hinge's rebranding as a relationship app appears to reflect a larger cultural trend. Notably, I'm coming across more and more couples who met on Tinder, despite the app's mostly hookup-y rap. One recently married Tinder couple had actually crossed paths several times over a period of years due to a complex network of mutual friends and roommates, but somehow had never gotten together until the timing was right — and so was the swipe. (Ironically, forward-thinking, technology-driven Tinder couple chose a musical throwback, "The Look of Love" for their first dance.) And one of the tightest aged twentysomething couples I know (and love) met on Hinge. Perhaps my relationship-seeking patients, friends, and relatives who prefer Tinder and Hinge to the other approximately nine hundred apps out there are really onto something different after all.

Coffee Meets Bagel

Regarding Hinge's newish focus on authentic connections, ditto for Coffee Meets Bagel, a dating app launched by three sisters who emphasize "quality over quantity." These female founders also added a unique twist to the site stemming from their claims that men enjoy browsing through lots of photos (I agree), versus women, who don't want to waste time in finding a relationship. Brilliantly, the sisters listened to women: female users are greeted on their phones with up to roughly six contacts or "bagels" per day based on basic Facebook profile information as well as brief answers to questions regarding school, occupation, enjoyable activities, and what you appreciate in a date, to name a few. Additionally, fun fact "ice-breaker" questions are included to, well, break the ice with app-suggested matches.

What's more, matches aren't offered to women unless the men already "like" her, short-circuiting potential unrequited interest — as well as instant rejection. According to one sister-founder, Arum Kang, a Harvard Business School graduate, as quoted on Xconomy.com, "That person is looking at your profile at the same time as you're looking at theirs. It's different than when you're one of many and you don't know who is looking at you." Kang continues, "[P]eople really look forward to the noontime e-mail to see who they are going to get." Looking even further forward, an internal survey of over five hundred users revealed that 67 percent of the men (and 79 percent of women) reported they're looking for a serious relationship or spouse.

JSwipe

But even Coffee Meets Bagel doesn't match people based on religion: enter JSwipe, sometimes referred to as "Tinder for Jews." Various women claim that the men they've met on JSwipe are less hookup hungry than Tinder matches — kosher intentions, shall we say. Women also mention that they feel like they're no longer competing with the "teeny-tiny black dress/bikini" crowd. Then again, if you're a nice Jewish girl, or any genuinely nice girl for that matter, who rocks a party dress with the best of them, you *are* the competition. Mazel Tov.

Bumble

So far, here's the buzz on (relatively) recently launched Bumble. Primary advantage: women are required to start the conversation with their matches. Primary disadvantage: women are required to start the conversation with their matches. And all this within twenty-four hours of both users swiping right or the match disappears. (That being said, men can opt to extend one match per day by twenty-four hours. Meaning that if he does, he's either in denial about his chances, or super interested in his choice—probably both.)

As for the good news, women don't have to subject themselves to tons of ridiculous, lewd messages involving crudely referenced private body parts, and even cruder acts. And Bumble's users tend to be slightly better educated and more career-oriented than Tinder's, whose user base encompasses a broader spread of people. But some of my patients complain that the men they communicate with seem to be less assertive than they'd like, perhaps a self-selected effect of choosing an app where women make the first move. Overall, however, Bumble may be the most female-empowering of the bunch. Which makes sense, considering founder Whitney Wolfe created the app after an acrimonious, litigious breakup with her boyfriend whom she had worked alongside marketing a company he cofounded. And the name of the now-competitor company? Tinder.

The Matchup: Which Men Use Which App

App	**Type Guy**
Tinder	Hookup Guy Sometimes Falls in Love
Hinge	Deeper Guy Open to Relationship
Coffee Meets Bagel	Serious-Minded Guy Who Likes You
JSwipe	Nice Jewish Guy Seeks Future Wife
Bumble	Career-Oriented Guy Seeks Alpha Female

When to Meet after the Initial Contact

There's an initial "intimacy" that develops between digital matches via the sharing of personal information before actually meeting IRL (in real life). Perhaps that's why Finkel's review of four hundred online dating studies found that a few weeks of texting and exchanging pictures with your newfound match is optimal to intensify the attraction once you actually meet. However, such correspondence can backfire in terms of inflated expectations and accompanying disappointment if it continues for six weeks or longer. A female "serial" Tinder user nailed it in a *Guardian* interview: "When you're matched, you can spend days – in some cases, weeks, months – exchanging messages, texting and working yourselves up, filling in the gaps with your imagination. By the time you meet, you've both invested so much, you've raised your hopes and his." That's precisely what happened to twenty-nine-year-old nurse Lyndsey; she couldn't wait to meet a Match man she'd been chatting with for several weeks. But what a buzzkill when, in Lyndsey's words, "this gross guy" showed up looking nothing like she'd imagined from his pictures. So I recommend waiting about two to three weeks max from initial contact to first date to heat things up, but know that much more than that may ultimately lead to a hope-plummeting cold burst of reality instead.

Falling for a (Virtual) Stranger: Online Relationships

In addition to using online dating sites and smartphone apps to find people to date in person, the Internet has provided all sorts of new arenas for romantic-ish (with emphasis on "ish") encounters. The gamut runs from men and women who message lots of different people in an attempt to find connection, or cheap thrills, or a brief online-only relationship — to full-on obsession. But what the entire continuum of online relationships have in common is: whether it's a cyberspace connection with a total stranger (such as through Internet gaming or online forums), or online correspondence highlighted by frequent back-and-forth emails or texts with someone you know (or a "virtual" unknown), the immediacy, ambiguity, and sometimes anonymity of Internet interactions elicit considerable emotional openness. The almost trancelike, meditative mindset of many Internet musings feels similar to writing in a personal journal or diary and is similarly conducive to disinhibited self-disclosures that would never happen that quickly, if at all, in face-to-face interactions. That's where you look at something you wrote later and think: "I can't believe I sent that."

Those regrets surfaced during therapy with Paige, a forty-one-year-old corporate attorney. During a course of copious back-and-forth messaging over two or three weeks with an attractive new cross-country Facebook friend (whom she digitally "met" through a close colleague), Paige wrote that she gets turned on fantasizing about "bringing down" a recent ex who broke up with her shortly after discovering she hacked his phone. To make matters worse, Paige followed that bombshell with, "I think I'm falling in love with u." No shocker when Paige never heard from the guy again. (Incidentally, I advised Paige to stick to journaling for her fantasies next time, not Facebook messages.)

It helps to understand that psychologically, online relationships can be just as seductively compelling and powerful as regular relationships. For women, flirtatious online banter as well as weightier sharing of feelings may signal at least a deep friendship, if not something more. In contrast, men associate friendship and romance with getting together IRL; for them, online relationships are mostly meaningless. Women in particular are especially susceptible to becoming "addicted" to online relationships; they get the same rewarding surge of pleasure-activating neurotransmitters that they do in enjoyable face-to-face interactions. The same goes for your iPhone: that happy, hopeful "ping" signaling a text—from *him*—is like a sweet shot of sugar to your brain. But please be aware, ladies, that even the cutest emojis are no substitute for facial expression, body language, intonation, and pitch, which linguists estimate constitute at least 70 percent of the meaning we derive from in-person encounters. Surprisingly, a mere 30 percent of perceived meaning is actually based on what we say.

Also, recent research has shown that people tend to lie the most through text messages, followed by emails, compared with face-to-face or over the phone. People have more time to word their lies, typically in a self-serving manner, when texting and emailing. Additionally, the sender realizes he won't immediately see your reaction when hurting you or doing something wrong. And of course men and women alike are both equally vulnerable to cyber-problems, a.k.a. "stuff" people do online. Anyway, if your laptop is getting more action than your man's lap (!), then it may be time to figure out why. Overall, caution and discretion are key, so to speak, in engaging in Internet relationships (Facebook friend or faceless poser?), particularly if you've had limited in-person contact with your new Internet buddy. Or if you don't really know him at all.

X-Posed Sexts — Just Say No

Finally, sexting, or the sending or posting of sexually explicit messages, photographs, and videos via mobile phone or computer, as tempting as it may be, is recklessly risking far more exposure than you ever bargained for. Bottom line: when it comes to getting naked digitally — don't. Even for trusted boyfriends. No matter how much he begs for a topless selfie or you can't wait to show off your new nipple ring. Unless, of course, you don't mind appearing on a porn site, which is where, according to Internet Watch Foundation estimates, 88 percent of self-made explicit photos "stolen" from an original download location ultimately end up. Keep in mind that your digital footprint (and I'm not talking toes) is here to stay, so don't become a victim of your own naiveté.

Step 6 Playlist ♫
All About That Bass/Meghan Trainor
Cupid/Sam Cooke
The Look of Love/Burt Bacharach, Hal David

What a wicked thing to do, to make me dream of you . . .

— Chris Isaak

Step 7

Light His Fire: Why He Can't Stop Thinking About You

Too many women today self-sabotage their chances of a romantic connection with men they're attracted to by acting, well, like guys. They fast-track new dating partnerships sexually, but, unlike many of the men with whom they sleep, they're truly disappointed when an actual relationship doesn't follow. The quick sex is a lot like instant coffee: the jolt is there, but no one cares. Ahh, but how we're seduced by the intoxicating aroma of a *slow* brew. Similarly, mutual attraction left to percolate and anticipate just grows hotter and hotter. In contrast, misguided, cloying attention early on or aggressive sexual overtures on the part of women (and actually men as well) ironically only serve to effectively extinguish whatever flicker of desire may have been there in the first place. Don't just take my word for it: using blockbuster new technology, researchers have unraveled the science of attraction, revealing how to "get into his head" — and stay there.

The Neuropsychology of Romantic Love

Think about the language of love: we "fall" madly in love; we are "crazy" in love; we are "lovesick"; love is "blind." Okay, you get the idea. What all these phrases have in common is the idea of an irresistible force drawing us to the object of our desire so that we will do anything and everything in our power to be with them. The attraction puts us in a highly aroused state to the point that we may lose our appetite and have difficulty sleeping and concentrating — actually, the only thing we seem to be able to concentrate on is figuring out when we're going to see that person next. This happens as our brains experience a seesaw increase in the neurochemical pleasure-messenger dopamine with a simultaneous drop in the calming mood stabilizer serotonin. Behavioral translation: obsessive phone calls and texts of the "I miss you/am thinking about you" variety. And let's not forget about often impaired, lust-fueled judgment.

There is an emotional urgency and intensity integral to this neuropsychological attraction that's driven by an all-encompassing biological undertow. This strong, forceful attraction additionally causes an amphetamine-like chemical known as phenethylamine, or PEA, to be released by the brain, which generates a temporary rush of euphoria. That's why PEA is referred to as the "love drug"; its effect on the reward center of the brain is nearly as powerful as what makes a drug addict crave another line of cocaine. So all that a hopelessly smitten soul can do is seek out his next intoxicating "fix" of PEA — which he only gets from seeing you! This is what constitutes the true chemistry of attraction — in other words, the Holy Grail of dating. Kings have given up thrones, and presidents have thrown away legacies when they've experienced this kind of chemical attraction. Sometimes love is sudden and catches one unaware, as in "love at first sight." Similarly, when a man says that a woman simply "knocked me out," the attraction is instantaneous. But in countless other cases the chemistry or sexual attraction builds. At least if you let it.

Jeff is a thirty-six-year-old realtor who had never paid much attention to a particular receptionist, Ann, at the escrow company he uses. As Jeff put it, "This 'smokin'' redhead started to really pour it on — being very flirtatious — all over me." At the very least, flirting signals to a man that a woman finds him attractive somehow, which, as with Jeff, immediately gets his juices flowing. But instead of letting their newfound mutual attraction pick up some steam, Jeff and Ann slept together right away. Although it's been a few weeks and they're still dating, Jeff is not nearly as red-hot for his redhead as initially.

Flirting as a Turn-on (Versus a Turnoff)

According to scientists, flirting enhances chemistry between people if there is even a minuscule amount of attraction to begin with. The actual psychological crux of what makes flirting feel so good is that it has the potential to release dopamine, that phenomenally pleasurable neurochemical, in our brain. In fact, if it isn't welcome and pleasant for *both* parties it's not flirting per se, which is precisely what so many insensitive men who make sexually charged comments to female colleagues and underlings alike apparently don't understand. (Left unchecked such comments and "compliments" can easily deteriorate to the level of harassment.) So if his attempted flirting makes you uncomfortable, by all means cut if off at the start by saying so.

But assuming you're into the guy, researchers from the University of Nevada's Department of Psychology reported in *Sex Research* that for women, being desired can be a huge turn-on in and of itself. (And that applies whether you're a femme fatale or fateful feminist—or both.) This also confirms some women's claims that at the beginning of a relationship, being chased after is actually more pleasurable than sex. Armed with an understanding of the science of attraction, *any* woman can turn up the heat with her man of choice.

> *You can't start a fire without a spark*
> — Bruce Springsteen

FLIRT with New Skills

F Firsts
L The Look
I Intimacy
R Rock It
T Touch and Tease

Flirtatious FIRSTS

Think about what initially motivated you to read this book. My guess is that it was a quick look at the title, a glance at the cover, or a perfunctory read of the introduction or table of contents. You immediately were hooked; otherwise, you would have passed on reading further. Analogously, flirtatious firsts entice a man to desire more — of you.

Perceptually, all firsts register a lasting imprint on the brain. A first impression is actually a *permanent* impression: it's the one that is going to stick. Take your clothing, for instance. Your clothes are your packaging; what you wear makes an immediate, strong statement about you. When on a first date particularly, make sure you wear something you know you look and feel good in. If that means buying a new outfit, go for it; but the best "shopping" is often done in one's own closet.

Or simply buy a truly transformative pair of shoes that look amazing and perk up almost anything you wear. Hopefully they're heels. A study that appeared not in *Vogue* or *Elle*, but in the academic journal *Evolution and Human Behavior*, found that the same women walking in a video were rated significantly more attractive (by both sexes) in heels than in flats. I'd have presumed that's because heels elongate the leg; however, the researchers found through biomechanical analysis that wearing high heels emphasizes feminine aspects of gait such as increased hip rotation and tilt, which actually triggers sexual arousal in men. (Side note: men's jean-clad hips do it for us.) Independently corroborating the study results closer to home, one twentysomething-year-old recently explained to me that a dating partner he "likes a lot" but wishes he were more attracted to "never wears heels." Interestingly, despite limited utility for actual walking, high heels have endured over time reportedly because they emphasize "sex-specific" features. Similarly, many heels' knockout heights parallel their sky-high prices (think: Christian Louboutin), reflective of heavy demand. The same can't be said for other less female-friendly, mostly unpopular fashions such as shoulder pads, which have no sex appeal whatsoever.

What else isn't appealing is overkill. Therefore, you may wish to save that cute, trendy animal print minidress for the second or third date where it won't be forever etched into your guy's brain. Quietly provocative tends to be much more seductive than outfits that scream "look at me." Less really is more; that holds for jewelry as well. Chemistry is all about sex appeal, so regardless of what you have on, you want to *feel* sexy. Even if your go-to wardrobe standbys are completely buttoned up, wearing beautiful lingerie that your date won't see — at least not yet — can make you feel sexy and attractive, which gets expressed outwardly. Remember, you're going on a date, not a job interview. Once again, it's demeanor and attitude that can make a conservatively dressed woman much hotter than her bare-to-there counterpart.

Along these same lines, don't make the mistake of equating a sexy manner of dress with being sexually available. This is tantamount to saying that a rape victim was "asking for it." A low-cut blouse or short skirt at any age says that the wearer is attuned to her body and femininity; it says nothing about if and when she'll have sex. Or, as women carrying signs at a recent Los Angeles event to promote "outrage toward derogatory labeling and victim blaming," among other issues, more eloquently put it: "My clothes are not my consent," and "The way I dress does not mean yes." This sentiment was forcefully echoed by former Vice President Joe Biden, who in October, 2015 vehemently admonished nationwide college students as part of his "It's On Us" campaign, "It is *never, ever* appropriate to ask a rape victim what she was wearing." Since too many men out there apparently don't yet "get" this message, use common sense. For example, it's not wise to flaunt cash, jewelry, or skin when alone in unfamiliar surroundings. But even parading in the skimpiest of bikinis on the beach doesn't mean that you owe the men lusting after you sex. Just get really good at saying no.

In fact, given your rocking female anatomy, there are some instances where you're going to have to fend off unwanted sexual advances regardless of how you dress. Especially if you're in the military: best available Pentagon survey data reveals as many as 26,000 cases of unreported sexual assaults of females, a significant two-year increase of 35 percent. To explain this troubling trend, former air force top commander, Gen. Mark Welsh III, appears to blame broader society, noting that 20 percent of women report they had been sexually assaulted "before they came into the military." In testimony before the Senate Armed Services Committee, he claimed: "They come in from a society where this occurs. Some of it is the hookup mentality of junior high even and high school students now, which my children can tell you about from watching their friends and being frustrated by it." At least he didn't blame the uniforms.

As for that first real kiss, be sure and let your partner be the one to make the move. After that, just enjoy it. If the guy's a keeper, that's one first that you truly do want forever embedded in both your brains.

The LOOK (In Your Eyes)

He's checking you out; you're checking him out. So what happens next?

If you really want to turn a man on, look him in the eyes—and keep looking. Sound simple? It's not. That's because most people automatically look away from someone's eyes after just a quick moment or two when we're talking. (Typically meeting the other's eyes averages only one to two seconds even between friends conversing.) Neuroscientists who study the chemistry of love specifically recommend holding a man's gaze for two-thirds of the time you two are talking, however, to fire up his brain's neurotransmitters—and him. Stepping it up, when nobody is speaking, hold your partner's (or soon-to-be partner's) gaze for just under ten seconds and then deliberately avert your eyes. A former Geisha patient of mine swears by that one. Backtracking a bit, even before any words are spoken, a glance signals interest. For instance, watch that random, cute guy smile (or more) when you tilt your head just so. Or try "nonchalantly" running your hand through your hair while glancing his way.

The emphasis is on the glance; it's his for the catching. Men have difficulty resisting the allure of a woman's flirty, captivating eye contact, which is arguably even more disarming than her beauty. Note that when thrice-married rock icon Rod Stewart was asked by an *LA Times* reporter in 2012 what he found sexy, this former dated-mostly-models womanizer responded, "It's in the eyes. I've been out with some extremely beautiful women who have had no sex appeal whatsoever. It really is a lot more than skin deep."

INTIMACY through Empathy

While "The Look" aims to allure, the cultivation of emotional intimacy strengthens and seals the attraction. In fact, flirting is in large measure so provocative because it carries the suggestion of a greater intimacy later on. And it's not just sexual intimacy. To quote a recent *Psychology Today* article: "Becoming close to another person is one of the most thrilling experiences in the human repertoire, both the bedrock of emotional security and a passport to self-expansion."

But how do you get there?

For starters, two people aren't going to get past even a promising but superficial connection if either is feeling unduly self-conscious, which is not all that unusual among new dating partners. So if you need to calm your own nerves, try focusing on *him*, with the unanticipated benefit of making a man you're attracted to feel as though he's the only person in the room. This involves rapt listening as your partner talks about his favorite subject: what else — himself. Don't worry; if the guy truly is interested he'll want to know all about you soon enough. But contrary to what many women believe, it's actually less about your attributes and more about how a man *feels* when he's with you that is going to be the determining factor as to where the relationship goes (or doesn't). The same holds true for you as well; it's largely how you feel when you're with someone that will determine whether you want them to hang around.

If strong, mutually pleasurable feelings are the building blocks of romantic attachment, then empathy is the cement. Empathy is defined as "the ability to understand and feel what someone else is feeling in an emotional sense." Men and women are both psychologically hardwired to desire connection with others; the more we feel understood and valued by a partner, the more connected we feel to them. As for basic human connection, romantic or otherwise, phrases like, "I really understand how you must have felt when that happened," or a simple "I get it" make anyone feel especially good. But don't fake it. Men, and everyone else for that matter, also respond very well to statements like, "Help me understand" or "I'm trying hard to understand how you must have felt in that situation." If empathy isn't your strong suit, you can nonetheless cultivate compassion and understanding by truly contemplating how you would feel in someone else's shoes, not just with your man, but in general.

Then again, if emotional understanding just isn't in your DNA, don't despair. Another way to foster intimacy is by personal disclosure; that is, telling a select guy something private about yourself or your life. And, oh yeah, be sure to mention that this is something you're confiding only to him. This happens very naturally as a relationship progresses.

In fact, those confidence-sharing, lose-track-of-time talks help propel early, heady romantic attraction before you really get to know someone into a tried-and-true romantic relationship. We become our loved one's cherished cheerleader, avid helpmate, and trusted confidante. And it's where life experience tends to teach us what really matters. As such, physical appearance, so important in the early stages of attraction, becomes eclipsed by attributes such as fidelity, loyalty, kindness, dependability, and intelligence, all of which are touted as paramount to long-term mating, according to University of Texas–Austin evolutionary psychologist David Buss, PhD. One more make-or-break relationship attribute I'd include: integrity. I'd also add good impulse control to that list as well, especially for unavailable women who are strikingly good-looking and for married men who are strikingly rich.

ROCK IT with Laughter and Playfulness

Yet another way to amp up attraction is by rocking your date with laughter and humor. Consider laughter as a first-date orgasm that can even override a lack of initial chemistry. And if you laugh together, preferably repeatedly, you may just have the start of a great relationship. But remember, a sense of humor, like confidence, doesn't develop overnight. No, you don't have to do stand-up, but please do start looking at the funny side of things. (To help you get your laugh on, I especially recommend both Amy Schumer's and Whitney Cummings's often hilarious if brutally heartfelt insights, which are especially relatable to women.)

To further drive home the power of laughter, consider the following from late twenty-five-year-old poet Max Ritvo who used humor even to deal with his own terminal cancer: "When you laugh at something horrible, you're just illuminating a different side of it that was already there. . . . It's a mnemonic device that makes our suffering rhyme with joy." Tragedies notwithstanding, I guarantee that if you look for humor in most situations, you'll almost always find it, and an added bonus may be that you stop continually looking at the bleak or worst side of things. Still, as renowned positive psychology researcher Martin Seligman, PhD, wisely notes, "You're never going to make a curmudgeon into a giggly person."

Yet you can have a good time trying. Once again, laughter provides a direct "hit" to the pleasure center of our brains (ventral medial striatum), so if your time together includes together-laughs, your date may not remember what was so funny—but he will definitely remember you.

Equally endearing is laughter's close cousin: playfulness. In addition to attracting the opposite sex, adults who are playful rate higher on measures of psychological well-being than their more restrained brethren. So please do be spontaneous, fun, expressive, creative, and/or silly—that is, playful—from time to time. Notably, some people who describe themselves as "very serious" are actually among those who most easily laugh at themselves and with others; approaching life in a serious, responsible manner does not preclude a lighthearted, joyful aura.

TOUCH and TEASE

Last but by no means least, touching and teasing are also integral to FLIRTing, and involve the body as well as the mind. If you happen to graze your guy's leg with your own leg while sitting together, or lightly touch his arm, just watch the sparks fly! Assuming a guy already finds you attractive, you'll trigger a lightning-bolt, exhilarating chemical rush in the pleasure center of his brain. Similarly, taking your finger and lightly brushing a few crumbs off his chin or wiping a beverage remnant from your date's lips is *seemingly* innocuous. Once again, if there's any sexual tension between the two of you, on-the-surface small gestures like these will come across as incredibly hot. Just don't go overboard.

Intriguingly, the fact that sensual actions, such as lightly grazing a guy's face with your finger, are not overtly sexual makes their erotic pull that much more powerful. But whether or not you choose to touch, don't forget the occasional tease; for instance, you might "accidentally" flash just the slightest bit of thigh as you enter your date's car. Or try flashing your thong, but only if you're prepared to deal with the consequences. Monica Lewinsky admitted under oath that she had raised her jacket and showed the president the straps of the thong underwear poking out from her pants just before President Clinton acknowledged their mutual attraction and asked if he could kiss her. (On a side note, Clinton's seemingly consent-seeking "ask" may be rendered meaningless given the wildly exploitative power dynamics involved.) Regardless, that calculated tease appeared to be a watershed moment ultimately leading to an American president's impeachment for the second time in history, not to mention years of humiliating notoriety for Lewinsky. A safer choice, cognitive or mental teasing can be just as hot as a visual tease but without compelling the guy to jump on it (literally). So don't hesitate to mention your surprise in the *shower* earlier in the day when your doorbell rang — or how yesterday's *bikini* shopping went. Feeding his fantasies, those sexy, "dope" images are catnip for guys' dopamine!

How to Get a Guy to Approach You

While in its totality FLIRT works well in a new or ongoing relationship, individual components are also effective when you're simply trying to get noticed. Notably, Researchers Monica Moore, PhD, and Diana Butler of Webster College observed "social situations conducive to male-female interaction" to determine which women were approached most often by men. They found that the women who were approached most often glanced around the room, smiled at a man, and patted or smoothed their hair. Other less frequent "approach" behaviors included, "short, darting glances at men, lip licking (hmm), 'dancing' in the chair, and head tossing." According to the researchers, women who rarely displayed any of those behaviors, instead focusing attention mostly on female companions, were hardly ever approached. Additionally, contrary to their expectations, Moore and Butler found that unattractive subjects (women were previously rated as attractive, average, or unattractive) who exhibited the above "display" behaviors were approached far more frequently than "low-displaying" attractive women. Just a little something to keep in mind the next time you wish to step up your game.

Flirting, Geisha-Style

Geishas are world-class flirts. At least they've got "The Look" and the conversational part down. Not to mention teasing and playfulness. Although originally geishas routinely performed one ceremonial act of paid sex (in which her virginity was lost), that practice was outlawed in 1959. From then on, true geishas entertained men, and sometimes women as well, exclusively with light conversation and highly honed performance arts such as music, dance, and poetry. As author Kenneth Champion notes, "[T]hey are truly the most impeccable form of Japanese art." Champion continues, "There is currently no Western equivalent for a geisha."

I'm not so sure.

The Western version of a geisha is a really good flirt. Japanese scholar K.G. Henshall states, "Geisha engagement may include flirting with men and playful innuendo; however, clients know that nothing more can be expected. In a social style that is common in Japan, men are amused by the illusion of which is never to be." Henshall's words cut to the core of what's often so challenging for the rest of us "non-Geishas" who are concerned that our flirting may be misinterpreted. Note that a "suggestion of greater intimacy down the line" is not a *promise* of greater intimacy. Meaning that in no way does flirtation give anyone, including dating partners, grounds to expect sex. As explained earlier, when it is welcome flirting frequently just feels great in and of itself. And of course, as will become painfully clear in the following section, even for mutually pleasurable "consensual flirting" the context is critical.

Flirting with Disaster: Married Men

It may come as a surprise that I have no problem with married women being flirtatious with someone other than their husbands (the resultant randy feelings can often enliven their own marriage), but only when the flirting goes no further. This stance isn't new: note that now-ninety-year-old iconic sex therapist Dr. Ruth first recommended flirting to married women at least thirty years ago. Not so, however, for single women with married men where both parties are ultimately aiming for far more than flirting.

This may resonate if your history of heartache has led you to sacrifice your scruples by telling yourself you "deserve happiness" at all costs, regardless of the human "costs" and however illusive that happiness may ultimately be. Statistically, fewer than ten percent of adulterous affairs result in marriage between the partners, in no small measure because the deception involved brings an avalanche of problems. Having illicit sex particularly that harms existing relationships is like building a house of cards on a dubious foundation of secrecy, betrayal, and guilt: its collapse is inevitable, no matter how tight the relationship may feel at the time. And know that your lover's wife isn't the only one being deceived. Even if she really is a "witch," or they "don't have sex anymore" or are no longer "in love," bottom line: he's *chosen* to remain married. (Kids and finances are two common reasons, and not necessarily in that order.) Regardless of how enraptured you two may be with one another, the above statistics predict your affair will not necessarily lead to anything permanent. Ditto for my practice's stats: all but one of more than a few patients over the years who've slept with married men ended up primarily with broken promises — and hearts.

Yes, it may be tough to resist the urge to reciprocate the attention of someone unavailable (and desirable) who is pursuing hard. That said, reality, reason, and recognizing what's right will hopefully curb the temptation. But if he's single and cute: go for it. FLIRTing at the very least will get you noticed or raise the stakes on an already existing attraction.

Unless, of course, you manage to mess up in one of several ways that guys say turn them off no matter how strong the chemistry is.

Top 10 First-Date Deal-Breakers
Don't:

1. Criticize his appearance or his car, even in jest. Sounds like common sense? Apparently not. I had one patient who remarked to her date upon first seeing his car, "You're not really taking me out in *that*?" Another told a blind date she thought he'd be taller. Later, both women couldn't understand why the men didn't call.
2. Belittle him for his chivalry. A friend of mine reported that as he was opening the car door for his date, she

remarked that she could do that for herself because, "I'm not handicapped." True. But she did handicap the date, which was their first — and last.

3. Talk incessantly about yourself. This is a date, remember, not a therapy session. Don't panic if there are some silences; these can be expected. Also, try to keep up on at least some major current events. Besides showing interest in the world around you, you'll have an easy way to fill in gaps if conversation loses flow.

4. Partake of excessive alcohol or questionable substances — that is, drugs — before your date, no matter how nervous you are. You want to be yourself, not an altered version of yourself. Also, please don't get drunk on the date! Besides having sexual implications that are best avoided at the very outset of getting to know someone, it's just all-around unattractive. A good rule of thumb is to not order more drinks than he does; in fact, fewer is preferable.

5. Order the most expensive item or items off the menu (even if you're going out with the CEO of a small country). Your date will feel taken advantage of, no matter how much money he has; I guarantee it. And honestly, isn't that what you're really doing? So play it safe and choose an item that is no more expensive than what he orders. Along these same lines, don't name the most expensive restaurant or bar in the city when your new man asks for date suggestions.

6. Ask the guy how much money he makes. Ever. Similarly, don't interrogate your date about his job in a manner that makes it seem you're primarily interested in how much money he makes or how prestigious a position he holds. Note that I used the word "interrogate," which is typically applied to getting information out of criminals, spies, or terrorists. This is very different from friendly questioning about his work, which is encouraged.

7. Inundate him with questions about other women he's been with, whether relationships or women he's casually dated. Take the cue as to what he's comfortable discussing

from him. Do, however, find out whether he's separated or divorced right off the bat.

8. Complain about your job, family, and/or exes, including boyfriends and husbands. Consider this as the wrong "Double D," meaning it's a "date-downer."

9. Offer to pay for yourself, or, even worse, for both of you. Even though your date may not mind, it sets a precedent and implies friendship versus romance. Similarly, if a guy asks you to split the bill on a first date, no matter how broke he may be, you may as well split off romantic hopes for him as well. (Not so in an ongoing relationship, where it's considerate to pitch in for dates at least sometimes.) Finally, and this is the most important DON'T of all:

10. Sleep with the guy on the first date. Unlike most of the other Top 10 deal-breakers, your dating partner may in fact, call you again (because now his "bedsheets smell like you"), but it will most likely be a booty call.

Step 7 Playlist ♫
Wicked Game/Chris Isaak
Dancing in the Dark/Bruce Springsteen
In Your Eyes/Peter Gabriel
Shape of You/Ed Sheeran

I had hoped that you'd see my face and you'd be reminded
That for me it isn't over

— Adele

Step 8

Letting Go: When and How to Move On—or Move In

It's not just you.

Agonizing over whether or not you're going to hear back from some guy you've just starting dating is all too common. This is because when it comes to women, men's veracity frequently evaporates; in other words, men lie. A lot. They tell you that they're going to call, and then they don't. Men report that they do this to avoid "hurting women's feelings," but what they really seek to avoid is an explanation of why they don't want to see you again. All too often, this leads to never-ending guessing games of the "What is he *really* thinking?" variety. And then there are those frustrating times that you reach out first, and as my patient Alexia put it best, "He does that thing where guys ignore all your texts."

One of the most common concerns that arises among single women is how to navigate the aftermath of those first several dates, regardless of who is—or isn't—into whom. And if the two of you do hit it off and establish an intimate, ongoing relationship, you may eventually be faced with the question of whether to move in together. I'll share some eye-opening survey findings later on that will help you decide. At the opposite end of the spectrum is determining what went wrong (and getting through the pain) when a long-term boyfriend who wouldn't commit to you is suddenly engaged to someone else.

What to Say When You're Not into Him

Remember one of the first things you were taught as a child? Say thank you. If you don't wish to see a man again, a simple "thank you" at the end of a date will suffice. This is the decent thing to do, and the brevity of your words, together with a polite-but-cool tone of voice, should convey your disinterest. Nevertheless, if he says he wants to see you again, then a firmly stated "I don't think so" with or without explanation should send a disappointing (and disappointed) date packing. Remember, you don't owe the guy an explanation for your rebuff. In fact, often it is best *not* to explain, because that way there's no opportunity for a single-mindedly determined man who doesn't respect boundaries to try and persuade you by debating your reasons. There's a huge difference between a would-be dating partner being endearingly persistent and being flat-out wrong for you.

For example, a nice guy who "keeps trying" and treats you really well may warrant a second look. Similarly, turning someone down based on gut instinct is not the same as giving a man a chance even though you don't immediately visualize yourself hanging from the chandelier with him. But say you're totally put off or creeped out by someone who hits on you, then don't hesitate or hedge in your response. The same holds for that sketchy guy you've been dating awhile; trust your instincts. Some especially arrogant men believe they're automatically entitled to your acquiescence, whether in response to going out — or sleeping together — so the more direct and emphatic your "no," the tougher it will be to ignore. For most guys, anyway. There may be a particularly stubborn stonewaller at whom you need to fire a point-blank "We're done now." And if this tone-deaf dude still doesn't get the message, here's a foolproof way to get guys to back off: tell them you have a boyfriend.

Letting Him Know You're Interested: The New "Textiquette"

In a far happier example, if you wish to continue dating a new man, in addition to your end-of-date, warm verbal thank you, do send a short text letting him know that you had a great time. Not only do men report that such a message is an effective, understated way for a woman to convey her interest, but they often feel that women are unappreciative of their efforts if they don't meet this minimum post-date expectation. Consider the thank-you text message as part of the new dating textiquette. Also, if a man truly put an uncommon degree of initiative into planning and executing the date — for example, a long drive to pick you up, or a particularly creative or fun (okay, even pricey) venue — then a clear communication of gratitude makes him feel it (and you) were worth it.

Keep it short and sweet: guys uniformly advise not to send more than one or two brief texts whether or not they contact you within a day or two after an initial date. Regardless of how you deliver the message, if a man is interested in you, it stokes his ego to know he gave you a wonderful time.

An added plus for you is that your gratitude makes him want to please you even more. Any good businessperson knows that thanking someone is the best motivator; in fact, studies have shown that "thank you" correlates with higher profits. The same holds true for romantic "profits" (i.e., sexual pleasure), as demonstrated by a unique psychosocial study that found that people who expressed gratitude more than doubled their chances of being on that happy receiving end again. Incidentally, when it comes to sustaining a long-term relationship, a recent survey of Men'sHealth.com male readers found that 41 percent feel unappreciated. Perhaps not coincidentally, that is precisely the lifelong probability of American marriage ending in divorce (40 to 50 percent), estimated by PolitiFact.com. The take-home message: if you want to keep your man, let him know you appreciate him.

Why He Doesn't Call

Once you say thank you, it's time to just sit back and wait. Notice I didn't say sit back and fret, obsess, fixate, ruminate, call every friend you can think of and get their take on what's going on, or binge on chocolate (or whatever else you happen to have lying around your kitchen). In other words, don't overthink it. Okay, so this dude turned out to be a dud. As part of a sisterhood of "misery loves company," or more accurately *misery loves commiseration,* take solace in the fact that every woman on this planet has at some point fallen prey to at least one of the following:

---

10 Most Common Reasons Men Don't Call

- No chemistry
- Bad timing (someone else shows up/not relationship ready)
- Doesn't see it long-term (despite great sex)
- Not that attracted to you anymore
- Short attention span
- Getting back together with girlfriend
- Thrives on juggling multiple women ("harem-guy")
- Likes to hedge bets ("shopper")
- True player (this time it's *you* who should walk)
- Wants "perfect" woman (who doesn't exist)

Let's begin with chemistry. My own comprehensive study of nearly every online survey of why men say they don't call even though a first date seems to have gone really well involves chemistry. First, while you may have had a *great* time on the date, your partner had a good time — but not good enough to call you again. Perhaps you aren't his type, or the chemistry didn't happen for him. Men tend to describe this as a "spark" just not being there. If that's the case, odds are your first date with the guy will also be your last.

Another common reason for men bailing, even after several mutually enjoyable dates, is timing. A guy may indeed like you, at least for the moment, but someone else steps into his life whom he likes a lot more. (Sorry, but that's the truth.) Bad timing also includes guys who are really into you but are currently not in the market for a girlfriend. For example, a man may be attracted to you, but he wishes to date very casually or superficially at present (including casual sex). Sensing that you seek a serious relationship, he decides to cut things off right from the start. However hurtfully confusing at the time, this is often for the better to avoid deeper conflicts much further along the relationship road. As will be apparent in Step 9, timing is especially critical for men in terms of choosing to commit to a bona fide relationship.

Danielle, was convinced she'd found "her person" on their first date. It seemed perfect. She was a third-year dental student; he had just bought a dental practice. He was "smart, successful, and funny," and so was she. After dinner at a trendy beachfront restaurant, they went for a stroll along the boardwalk talking and laughing for hours. Their moonlit kiss (only) was "magical." It seemed like destiny was finally calling.

Wrong.

Not only did destiny not call, but neither did her date. As in, she never heard from him again. Nothing. Nada. Not even an "I had a great time, *but* . . ." text. Not even a put-her-out-of-her-misery response to Danielle's pride-plundering texts. After she was finally ready to stop beating herself up over her "misread," Danielle became, if not happy, at least comfortable with the confusion. My guess is that the guy's disappearance had something to do with timing/not being ready for a real relationship. Along with being an undercover jerk. But the harsh reality is that Danielle very likely will never know.

Then there's that guy you've been seeing for a while who does want a keeper-girlfriend yet still ends a budding relationship fairly abruptly. Yes, he does know exactly what he wants, and he also knows that it's not you. Nevertheless, these guys are conflicted about splitting because, put simply, the sex is good. (His take: "Trying to tell you no, but my body keeps on telling me yes.") In stark contrast, once a man's romantic desire for you wanes, including but not limited to the physical component, he'll often break things off more easily by saying, "You're too good for me" or equally frequently, "I don't deserve you." Guy translation: "You're a really nice person who treats me well, but I want a relationship that excites me." Another version of this is the tried-and-true platitude: "It's not you; it's me." Read (the real truth): "It's not your fault that I'm not all that attracted to you anymore." As dating prophet and author Greg Behrendt so insightfully observes, "Men would rather be trampled by elephants on fire than tell a woman 'I'm just not that into you.'"

There's also the unfortunate scenario where, unbeknownst to you, your date is already involved with someone else whom he's taking a break from. ("Break" meaning time out — or separation as an excuse to see other people.) So in essence, you (and others) may merely serve as fun, dispensable distractions while some girl's bad boyfriend decides whether to get back with her. Equally hurtful is the man who doesn't necessarily have a significant other in the wings, but he enjoys variety and thrives on the adrenaline rush of dating/juggling several women simultaneously. He readily recognizes your monogamous leanings — leading him to distance himself from you (and harems aren't your style anyway). A slight variant of harem-guy is the "shopper" who isn't necessarily into having sex with many women, but he nevertheless dates — and drops — several at the same time in order to hedge his bets at finding his own soul mate. When he suddenly stops asking you out or returning your texts, you know that you've been eliminated from contention.

Yet another reason why the guy you've recently been seeing stops calling is that you very possibly have encountered the true "player," or the inordinately charming but duplicitous Lothario who very quickly charmed the pants off you. Since a player's primary motivation is his own sexual gratification (as explained in Step 3), he will say and do anything to get you into bed. But it's only a matter of time before the true player cools off and disappears, despite how strongly he initially came on to you. (I had one patient report that a guy told her on their first — and only--date he could "sense" she was his soul mate.) So while you're crushed wondering what happened, this practiced liar is already targeting his next sexual conquest.

And although men won't admit to this in surveys, there are those who predictably cut women loose after a number of dates because they are continually looking for someone "better." Not a woman who provides a *better fit* for them; rather, they are searching for that "someone else out there" who always seems to elude them somehow. But how can you ever compete with an impossible-standard illusion? Think of confounding new men like puzzles with missing pieces. You wouldn't be able to complete a puzzle like that, nor can you figure something out when you don't have all the necessary information. So stop wasting your precious time and mental energy overthinking a deadbeat date: forget about the guy and move on.

Going Fishing: Your Next Text

If you absolutely can't resist sending him "just one more" email or text, even when you haven't heard from him in days/weeks/months, then once again remember: less is more. Here are some suggestions for what to say — as well as what *not* to send — insofar as "fishing" messages.

"Fishing" Texts: Dos and Don'ts

Do Send:

- Hey
- Heyyy ;) (flirtier version of above)
- Hi :)

- What's up?
- How are you doing?
- How did that (fill in the blank with: meeting, presentation, paper, etc.) ever go?
- Haven't heard from you in a while—are things okay?

Do Not Send "Desperation" Texts Such As:

- I haven't heard from you in ages—what's going on?!!!
- I miss you sooo much.
- I am really hurt.
- I AM HAVING A SERIOUS MELTDOWN: CALL ME
- It feels like forever since we talked . . .
- Why the #$%& haven't you called?!

Could Go Either Way:

- I have tickets to_____; would you like to come as my guest?

While it's fairly obvious how writing a guy saying you are having an all-caps "meltdown" would be off-putting, asking someone out whom you haven't heard from in a while is far dicier. Men have mentioned that they don't like this approach because it "forces" a response from them if they aren't interested in a woman. However, if a guy is merely ambivalent or needs a push, then providing an opportunity to see one another could be advantageous. Bottom line on that one is to use discretion.

When You Didn't See It Coming: The Blindside

Whereas absence of chemistry or out-of-sync timing often throw a man and woman off the relationship track early on, miscommunication is typically responsible for the blindsided breakup when two people have been dating for a sustained period of several weeks or months. Almost inevitably this is about the woman believing — or convincing herself — that a relationship is more serious than it is. To illustrate, in a second season episode of the concluded but iconic, trail blazingly true-to-life HBO sitcom *Girls*, a man offers to pay the woman he's been dating (and sleeping with) for helping him host a professional event. When the woman refuses the money, saying that he doesn't need to pay her because she's his girlfriend, he responds, "I didn't know I *had* a girlfriend." Writer-director Lena Dunham explains that there's always "that girl" who thinks the guy is her boyfriend, but he doesn't feel the same way about her. How true. Think DUMB: **D**istorted, **U**nspoken, **M**isleading, **B**otched communication. And DUMB dating leads to dumping!

But being dumb or clueless in a relationship (and equally dumbfounded when it abruptly ends) isn't necessarily your fault, especially when there are misleading communications on the part of your partner. *However awkward, the "What are we?" talk is not only appropriately assertive, but it helps to clarify where a relationship is — or isn't — headed.* Unless your partner manipulates you into believing he's more serious about you than what he really feels. In that case, if you suspect that you're playing DUMB, keep in mind that actions really *do* speak louder than words. For example, as in my patient Amy's case, although her boyfriend never hesitates to toss out an "I love you," a cross-country trip to visit a recent ex-girlfriend (whom he conveniently "forgot" to tell her about) suggests a blithe take on love. Anyone can say "I love you"; but as will be apparent in Step 9, how he shows it is what counts.

Excuses, Excuses: Boyfriends Who Won't Burn Bridges (Or Get Engaged)

In contrast to the quasi-serious relationship that's doomed from the start is the truly serious relationship that doesn't end well. For example, shortly after you break up, you may hear that a man you'd been dating seriously for several years has become engaged or married to someone else. Specifically, the two of you break up and then, boom! — he's engaged to someone new within a few months or a year. This is particularly painful if you had wanted to get married but your partner never would commit to you for the long haul. Unfortunately this is an all too common scenario, the aftermath of which often brings women into therapy to determine what went wrong. The most frequent reason that men give for their actions is that they never intended to make the woman a permanent fixture in their lives all along, but as time went on they became increasingly comfortable with the dating or living-together arrangement. These men sometimes confide in therapy that they "love" their long-term mates, but aren't "in love" with them.

The men in question also tend to say that although they "care about" their girlfriends, they can't envision or don't foresee a future with them. So these guys remain stuck, and their girl-friends ultimately end up as runners-up in what they describe feels like a commitment contest. Since the men don't want to say good-bye (true, they don't want to hurt you, but their real reasons are far more selfish), it's the women who eventually become frustrated and end the relationship. In essence, these are men who have great difficulty burning their bridges—but be forewarned, they will have no qualms whatsoever burning you should they encounter, even by chance, someone who jump-starts an all-new, all-consuming attraction. Thus, you may want to think twice before embroiling yourself further in a relationship where your partner is repeatedly dismissive of your hopes and dreams for the future. Remember, you have a rearview mirror too.

Note that there is a world of difference between being dismissive, which means that your partner refuses to even discuss an issue and consistently avoids it altogether, and just showing a degree of predictable trepidation or anxiety around the subjects of commitment or marriage, which are nevertheless tinged with a positive outlook. The challenge for many women is waiting out this sometimes confusing ambivalence among men. (My guess is if he's not at all attentive to your hopes for the future, he's also taking you for granted and not putting much, if any, effort into doing things that make you happy *now*.) But notwithstanding significant life stressors such as unemployment or severe illness, if a period of several years has transpired in an otherwise monogamous relationship where a woman's desire for matrimony is persistently ignored, discounted, or belittled, then an ultimatum may be in order. And know that, yes, in this circumstance when your partner unwaveringly states that he "doesn't want to get married," what he really means is that he doesn't want to get married to you. A man who has found the love of his life will do anything to keep her. "Anything" includes marriage.

If the above rings (sigh) painfully true, it's time to stop bemoaning the fact that you've reached an unenviable but inevitable end with a cowardly, commitment-averse partner. Most important of all, don't view the relationship as having been a waste of time. We all act based on information we have on hand; you based your very human path on love and optimistic hopes of a future together. You certainly didn't have a crystal ball predicting that your guy would ultimately let you down; thus the truism "Hindsight is twenty-twenty." Although it's tough to look ahead when your emotional wounds are still brutally raw, the experience will lead you to recognize and appreciate a truly great guy when he does come along. And that's when things stop feeling like a contest at all because you're number one in his life right from the start.

I counseled one patient, Lissette, who had believed her live-in boyfriend year after year when he explained why "this wasn't a good time to become engaged." She finally wised up—and worked up the courage to cut the cord after nine years of excuses. Within sixteen months of leaving the relationship, this forty-six-year-old woman was engaged to a wonderful man whom friends introduced her to; they now have a two-year-old son. So once again, it may be time to say thank you—in this case for the memories—and move on.

Broken Heart Syndrome (Yes, It's Real.)

Whether it's the bewilderment and frustration at being ditched early on by a promising new guy, or the shock and anger over the betrayal of a long-term lover, both scenarios have one important characteristic in common: loss. It is a well-known fact in psychology that the experience of loss is central to many major forms of depression, and loss is also the single best predictor of less severe episodes of depression as well. But for the first time in history, scientific research has credibly demonstrated why losing in love is one of the most painful losses there is. To illustrate, a cutting-edge 2012 UCLA study examined a group of 147 young women experiencing emotional pain ranging from social exclusion to bereavement. It was discovered that loss in the form of social rejection directed at and meant to affect a single person is the most devastating loss of all. The researchers even coined a name for this type of loss: "targeted rejection."

What this means in practical terms, for example, is that a person who is fired, or "targeted," experiences significantly more emotional pain than does a person who loses that same job, but as part of a larger group of coworkers who also lose their jobs at the same time. When it comes to dating, remarkably, the woman whose boyfriend breaks up with her (targeted rejection) may experience a more intense depression than if her boyfriend were to die. That is not to say that the latter instance of nontargeted "rejection" isn't also devastating, it's just processed differently by the brain. The newly revealed phenomenon of targeted rejection may help you understand the depths of your own despondency if and when you are unceremoniously dropped by a guy whom you mistook for your soul mate.

In fact, what woman hasn't been burned by a man somewhere down the line? And I really do mean "burned." Incredibly, brain scans analyzed by University of Michigan social psychologist Ethan Kross, PhD, revealed that people who were experiencing the emotional throes of a recent rejection by a romantic partner experienced activation in the same area of the brain (somatosensory cortex and dorsal posterior insula) as people who experienced the physical pain of a simulated burning sensation such as a scalding cup of coffee. In effect, both were truly burned!

It is truly remarkable that intense feelings of social rejection activate the exact same brain regions as physical pain; that doesn't happen with other emotions, such as anger. Separately, sometimes people experience sudden chest pains that mimic a heart attack simply when they're overcome by the pain of losing a partner or other loved one (i.e., instances of profound loss where rejection doesn't factor in). Mayo Clinic cardiologists explain that the heart may temporarily enlarge due to a surge of stress hormones, which are triggered by acute emotional pain. The cardiologists have even given a name to emotional heartbreak: stress-induced cardiomyopathy, or "broken heart syndrome."

Finally, if you've ever had a guy walk out the door (perhaps slamming it shut) after being called out on, say, his drinking or drug use, or if he abruptly announced that he was seeing someone else, your body was undoubtedly flooded with adrenaline, a stress hormone. A surge of "fight or flight" adrenaline causes increases in blood pressure and also increases in breathing rate, muscle contractions, and gastric symptoms such as cramps, nausea, vomiting, and diarrhea. (Also, feeling your stomach "drop" and "all the air sucked out of your body" are common.) These can be physical manifestations of severe anxiety, anger, or despair. If the stress becomes chronic (for instance, perpetuated by Facebook stalking and/or poring over hurtful Instagram shots of your ex and rebound girl), then the stress hormone cortisol will prolong various unsettling physical symptoms. So know that you are not "going crazy" when you experience an unwanted breakup with a man and then feel like you're falling apart, psychologically as well as physically. Although it may take a while to go from feeling like you can't live without him to "now you're just somebody that I used to know"; I promise that it does get better.

When You Can't "Shake It Off": How to Get Over Him

It's OK to not be OK — just don't stay there. Keep pushing.
— Mary Blige (referring to her ex's betrayal)

However disheartening an early rejection, or heart-wrenching a later breakup, it's important that you don't wallow in your pain endlessly. Sure, it's okay and even beneficial to indulge your misery — as in crushing disappointment and searing loneliness — for a week or two with bouts of crying. Tears themselves are actually neurochemically soothing, as are heartfelt, cathartic outpourings to your friends, especially the empathic ones. (Your BFFs particularly will wisely point out that the guy who you've been daydreaming down on one knee is totally unworthy of you.) Likewise, crawling back under your bed covers at inopportune times of day is comforting — for a while. Nevertheless, beyond a period of approximately four to six weeks, it's counterproductive to remain in a sad, melancholic state of mind not only because despair zaps your spirit and sanity, but also because of the danger of slipping into a debilitating depression. Particularly if that has been your pattern in the past or if a close family member has suffered severe depression.

While you want to recognize your feelings, don't think the unbearable emotional ache is going to last forever, a dysfunctional belief that positive psychologist Seligman has coined "permanence." Even just telling yourself that the pain isn't permanent helps. The saying "time heals" does hold true; on average, people stop experiencing classic grief symptoms (e.g., sadness, impaired concentration, numbness, crying spells, and joylessness) after six months. In the meantime, however, there are very specific things you can do to move the healing process along.

First and foremost, in order to avoid an insidious descent into Heartbreak Hell, catch yourself each and every time you begin to have negative thoughts; for example, that you're not "good enough," "unlovable," or that you'll "never" meet anyone you care about as much again. Counter these maladaptive thoughts by telling yourself that you are *more* than good enough and of course you are worthy of love (we all are). Most importantly, even though it's difficult to wrap your head around it in the moment, know that there isn't just one man out there whom you could ever feel strongly about. Similarly, if you begin to experience shame or humiliation, "talk" yourself out of these feelings by reminding yourself that they're a short-lived result of the rejection. In particular, don't get caught up in the "personalization" trap, which Seligman describes as believing we're at fault for everything that happens to us. With many guys (especially ones to avoid or even merely those with "missing puzzle pieces"), the relationship would have eventually shattered no matter what you did.

Following along positive psychology's upward trek, keep reframing your negative outlook through, at the very least, neutral, constructive thinking. Embrace each day as a new beginning, instead of with a sense of dread. This becomes much easier if you give yourself at least one thing to look forward to every day. (Cafe lattes work for me.) Hang in there, and eventually you'll notice your mood gradually beginning to lift.

In addition to the above modifications in your mindset, psychologists have recently uncovered simple actions that help heal emotional pain too. For example, keeping a journal or notebook of one's thoughts has credibly been demonstrated to diminish depression. So does guided or lucid dreaming, which involves visualizing the details of the dream you wish to have before you fall asleep. Also, begin to reengage in previously pleasurable activities; for example, if you typically enjoy movies, but just haven't felt like seeing any lately, push yourself to watch at least one. (But watching *Fatal Attraction* might be ill-advised.) As your ability to concentrate for longer periods improves, you'll find that distractions such as an engrossing film increasingly help you feel better — despite yourself.

Additionally, don't forget about friendships that you may have neglected during your relationship; research shows that time spent with good friends significantly elevates mood, an effect that lasts well past the duration of those visits. The same goes for truly appreciating those very friends and their kindness; such newfound gratitude may spill over to other parts of your life that are pretty wonderful, too. This positive awareness also guards against what Seligman refers to as "pervasiveness" or allowing one event (in this case a rejection or breakup) to affect all areas of your life.

As for those tears that keep breaking through, however cathartic crying may be, laughter soothes the soul as well. When you find yourself laughing again, it is as though you are re-entering life. Finally, strenuous working out, even if you build up to it gradually, releases the same pleasurable endorphins (a type of hormone) in your brain that sex does. All such proactive behaviors, along with persistent nixing of negative thoughts, will allow you to move on. Ultimately the hurtful rejection will elicit a different type of thank you to your ex, albeit delayed. This is because unlikely as it would have appeared at the time, his breakup afforded you the opportunity to find the genuinely *true* love of your life.

---

10 Best Heartbreak-Busters

- Reminding yourself that pain won't last forever ("permanence")
- Nixing of harsh self-judgement/self-blame ("personalization")
- "Talking" oneself out of shame/humiliation
- Embracing each new day as new beginning (look forward to something)
- Journaling
- Guided/lucid dreaming
- Reengagement in pleasurable activities
- Not letting breakup affect other areas of life ("pervasiveness")
- Visits with friends/daily dose laughter
- Strenuous workouts (releases endorphins)

Do You Move in with Him or Not?

Even if you're in a great relationship, you may wish to think twice before giving up your own place.

Specifically, during the course of therapy men and women both often discuss moving in with a particular partner, but express quite different concerns. Confirming my own anecdotal observations, a study conducted by University of Michigan researchers found that women view living together as part of a larger goal of a transitional arrangement preceding marriage. In contrast, men tend to consider cohabitation as a convenient, low risk way to see if a relationship has longer-term potential, using terms like "test drive" to describe the arrangement. Somewhat predictably, women interviewees volunteered "love" as a reason to live together three times more often than men, who cited "sex" as a reason four times more often. Women additionally believed that living together meant less commitment and legitimacy than marriage, while men saw the greatest disadvantage as a limitation on their freedom.

The women are definitely onto something.

Notably, a University of Denver research team examined nearly two hundred married couples' happiness and dedication levels based on their premarital history. The pivotal study found that men who had lived with their spouses before engagement were unhappier than men who cohabitated only after engagement or not at all. Furthermore, once married, these husbands were less dedicated to their wives than their wives were to them. Dedication here is defined as a strong, intrinsic desire to continue a relationship into the future. Of course we all know many mutually dedicated, happily married couples who lived together pre-engagement. So perhaps there's a different variable at play in the Denver study (such as the "cohabitation effect" described below) contributing to its more dismal findings.

Returning to the original question: How do you decide whether or not to move in with a man? If the two of you are highly invested in the success of the relationship, are planning an engagement or marriage in the foreseeable future, or at the very least are discussing a long-term future together, then go for it. Couples who live together do best (e.g., less fighting, less infidelity, higher reported happiness) when they have already made a strong, clear commitment to each other.

However, if you have noticed that your guy shows any ambivalence about the relationship, or about you, or if he has a "let's try this on for size" attitude, then don't. Otherwise all bets are off when you "notice" sexy texts from another woman in his phone, and you are back to apartment hunting — this time alone. Or, equally disturbing, you two may "slide" into a stifling marriage of convenience (e.g., to save money), with a statistically greater chance of divorce compared with couples who decide to cohabitate only after engagement or marriage. The University of Denver researchers refer to this as the "cohabitation effect," in which couples who live together get caught in a relationship inertia that eventually leads to a troubled marriage when they otherwise may not have gotten married. (Conversely, recent statistics show that if cohabitation is limited to one's future spouse with whom there are marriage plans all along, there is no increased divorce risk.) Cohabitation effect or not, some of my female patients attribute their own stubborn stay-put sensibilities in the midst of a less-than-happy live-in relationship to fear of change or being "alone," or both. Or they simply feel they've invested too much already to turn back.

Side note: What was once dreamt of as a magical ending can end up as a far grimmer chapter in the wrong fairy tale. Clearly, marriage is not a panacea. So if you're headed in that direction, it's best to ensure that as a pair both you and your future hubby have what it takes for the (very) long haul and are not just conveniently avoiding forging out on your own.

Step 8 Playlist ♫
Someone Like You/Adele
One More Night/Maroon 5
Somebody That I Used to Know/Gotye
Shake It Off/Taylor Swift

Part 3:

MAKING IT LAST: COMMITMENT, PASSION, AND SEX

'Tis but a kiss I beg
Why art thou coy?

— William Shakespeare

Step 9

The New Choice: Don't Sleep with Him Yet

sk your grandmother how many men she slept with before she met your grandfather. (Yes, you read that correctly.) I'm guessing it would be under ten, which is the average number of sexual partners you've fessed up to in polls. In all likelihood she may not have had sex with more than one or two men, if any at all, before she met your grandfather. She didn't have a choice; years ago women were expected to postpone intercourse until they were in a serious, committed relationship or, depending on religious or moral convictions, until marriage. While women typically associated sex with being in love, men equated sex with experimentation, fun, and eroticism. Essentially, men's inherent attitudes toward sex have remained mostly consistent with their behavior; they still enjoy sleeping with a variety of women but will shun them all when they meet a love interest, at least temporarily.

The problem is that for women there's now a major disconnect between their own innate feelings and culturally influenced behavior. Specifically, although today many women genuinely continue to experience intercourse as an expression of emotional closeness and caring, they often attempt to convince themselves that doesn't matter. Likewise, cultural mores and attitudes have evolved such that even the faintest trace of love is no longer viewed by many women as a prerequisite for sex. In some circles, commitment-based values and expectations regarding sex have been marginalized to the point that they have effectively fallen off the relationship radar altogether. Casual sex is readily acceptable and accessible by both sexes, with the gap obliterated between traditional gender roles (i.e., male aggressor; female gatekeeper), such that women are frequently the sexual initiators. To note, casual or recreational sex may be considered an expected part of dating, and it isn't unheard of for women to indicate desire for sex as a reason for dating.

Particularly among young women.

In a 2009 online survey of one thousand women by University of Texas–Austin psychologists, it was found that among aged twentysomething participants, many of the women reported having sex, or hooking up, purely for the experience and the adventure, or the desire to see what it was like to be with men of different ethnicities, or just to lose their virginity. However, *End of Sex* author Donna Freitas's nationwide college survey results underscore a far more disturbing side to hookup culture. She describes this underbelly in a 2013 *Washington Post* article as "oppressive" and "obligatory," with its "fast, uncaring, unthinking, and perfunctory sex. . . . [that] seems to leave students emotionally dulled or depressed about sexual intimacy and romance." Casual sex has also sprung forth a new wave of apathetic sexual participants of both genders — what Freitas dubs the "whateverists." Or, as I call it: the NBD-ers (No Big Deal). Referring back to the University of Texas study, it would logically follow from Freitas's findings that with repeated casual sexual liaisons, women will come to realize at some point that the "adventure" is wearing thin.

As a matter of fact, it's already happening. Nineteen and twenty-year-old women are coming to me depressed after "getting with" fairly random guys — lately after "popping a Molly or two." As a psychologist, I also work daily with people struggling with existential angst. Regardless of how elusive the answers may be, it appears that life's essence has at least something to do with meaningful, decidedly uncasual relationships. For instance, many hopeful young women I see in therapy today confide desires for deep romantic attachments and longings for boyfriends, some while simultaneously lamenting recent hookups. As one twenty-four-year-old patient related, "He is sooo hot, but now I wish I hadn't [hooked up]. He was already Instagramming pictures of himself and some blonde the next day." Or this from a Stanford sophomore: "I really didn't want to sleep with him yet, but he's older, and I was totally into him. Afterwards I mostly just felt used; I mean, c'mon—he wouldn't even spend the night."

Could I be witnessing a new psychological syndrome of "hookup fatigue" out there? Because for all that flying so high, there are far too many crash landings.

Turning Tides: Not Everyone Is Doing It

Perhaps somewhat surprisingly, given that hookup culture is highly visible in the bar/club/party scene and also tends to be widely hyped, sociologist Paula England's nationwide Online College Social Life Survey findings reveal that by senior year, four in ten college students are either virgins or have had intercourse with just one person. These students are just as much a part of popular culture as are their more sexually experienced peers, even though they typically aren't the ones out there broadcasting their sex lives. Consistent with England's data, a more recent survey of 26,000 American adults published in August 2016's *Archives of Sexual Behavior* found that millennials born in the early 1990s are 41 percent more likely to be sexually inactive than millennials born in the 1980s. Even more strikingly, the "Snapchat Generation" is more than twice as likely to be sexually inactive in their early twenties than first wave, 1960s-born Gen Xers were! And it's not just younger millennials that are increasingly foregoing casual sex. A 2008 OkCupid survey of its members found that 55 percent of men and 29 percent of women would date someone just for sex; remarkably, in 2017 those numbers dropped to 44 and 19 percent, respectively. All these solid statistics suggest the tides of sex and love are likewise turning toward a strong new wave of meaningful emotional intimacy versus ephemeral, fleeting pleasure. Then again, surface capricious currents may have never really affected deeper waters at all.

Regardless of philosophical underpinnings, what is vital for women to realize is that while fast, casual sex may still be encouraged through an unspoken code of conformity, it is not *mandated*. At the very least, that insight may give you pause if, like some young women whom I counsel, you believe you have to hook up to have any semblance of a social life. At its worst, blind conformity to a group standard leads to uninformed, regrettable cookie-cutter behavior. What's more, with today's #MeToo and Time's Up movements emboldening women to be much more upfront about their true feelings and concerns even when it comes to consensual sex, the clock may be ticking for casual hookups as a norm, too.

At the moment, however, since there are no longer any universally accepted rules of sexual conduct for women within a dating relationship, women are free to set their own standards, which are best informed by *knowledge,* not by whatever everyone else is, or seems to be, doing. A sociocultural mandate to treat sex casually or cavalierly can be just as oppressive as being forced into premarital abstinence. Your grandmother didn't have a choice: you, however, do.

How to Thrill in a 'Sex-on-Tap' Culture

Science supports what your mother may have shrewdly admonished: "Don't give it away." To illustrate, evolutionary psychology and social biology have long contended that for the human species to survive, men became hunters because breastfeeding women couldn't very well drag their babies along to stalk and kill animals to eat. Not only were men hunting wild animals, they were vying with other men for mating rights to limited numbers of women. There was an element of psychological thrill involved in both the survivalist (hunting) and reproductively competitive (mating) behaviors. And evolutionary psychologists know that while societal circumstances have clearly changed over thousands of years, the male of the species actually hasn't. Sure, now men don't depend on hunting for dinner — but they still like to hunt tail. So when women give a green light for sex too early on — sometimes even before it's asked for — they are taking away the thrill of the chase.

In a similar vein, the male patients I see who are searching for a serious partner sometimes complain that lovemaking with women they've just started dating is lacking somehow. And while the men do report a short-lived pleasurable surge, they confide that overall, sexual intercourse is no longer as exciting as it used to be when it was harder to come by.

Take the case of forty-five-year-old divorced NBA executive Greg, who is now in an exclusive relationship (sorry ladies). He recounted matter-of-factly that a few years ago he was sleeping with a different woman nearly every night of the week; nevertheless, he gradually found himself wishing he were home watching basketball on TV instead. It appears that many men today are becoming desensitized to sex; having it almost any time they want renders the experience less and less gratifying. (That's when hookup fatigue messes with guys, too.)

Somewhat less predictably, it's not just "older," more experienced guys that are becoming increasingly jaded about their sexual exploits. One teenage patient of mine recently quoted her eighteen-year-old boyfriend as saying he'd rather have "a meaningful relationship with no sex" than "lots of meaningless sex." Regardless of age, increasing numbers of men explain in one way or another that too much easily available sex "just isn't sexy anymore." It's like a person who eats chocolate all the time and eventually no longer finds it as delicious. (Interestingly, chocolate and sex both release PEA, or the "love chemical," into the brain.) Feminist author Naomi Wolf, in her essay "The Porn Myth," expresses similar sentiments: "[T]he power and charge of sex are maintained when there are some sacredness to it, when it is not on tap all the time."

As for how to remain exciting to a guy in a sex-on-tap culture, the key is his willingness to invest in a relationship. If a man is truly into you and is looking for something substantial, the positive challenge peppered with anticipation will override his frustration. Especially if you respond to a dating partner's pressure to sleep with you by telling him "no" straight out—at least for now. Once again, how far and how fast you go while perhaps drawing a line at intercourse is still up to you. But even if you move at a snail's pace, know that a really worthwhile, quality guy who is down for more than a short-term thrill won't walk away.

Sync Up with Your Psyche

In a healthy relationship, a man won't be able to keep his paws off you whether or not you've started sleeping together, but women don't typically experience the same touchy-feely urgency toward men. Think about it: What is the female equivalent of "blue balls"? Men and women are not psychological and sexual equals; any woman who pretends otherwise is just deceiving herself. Or she might be buying into popular cultural messages a tad too mindlessly.

For example, even if you do choose to engage in casual sex purely for kicks, or perhaps you seek (or miss) the lusty, lingering endorphin rush, at least be aware that quick hookups are out of sync with the female psyche. Psychologically, sex is rarely "casual" for women. In fact, when it comes to sex, men and women occupy two entirely different emotional demographics. Blame it on *your* brain, which unlike that of your non-childbearing male counterparts, has an evolutionary-based propensity for sexual-emotional attachment. We females evolved from our ancestral sisters, who had the best shot at birthing and raising viable offspring when securely paired up with sexual partners to ensure paternal care. That is one reason we continue to emotionally attach to men with whom we have intercourse; for women at least, a purely "physical relationship" isn't our default setting.

Not so for guys.

As Robert Martin, PhD, distinguished author of *How We Do It: The Evolution and Future of Human Reproduction* consistently notes, parenting by males, who neither carry nor nurse offspring, is not *obligatory*. Instead, nature deemed it in a male's genetic interest to spread his sperm among as many females as possible to increase the odds of having any progeny at all. Thus, men, who are reproductively fiercely competitive and also have strong, testosterone-fueled libidos, experience an astronomically high level of excitement when trying to sleep with you. He's engaged in a game of adult tag and you are it. But of course the game ceases to be as much fun if you are "tagged" right away.

Your Vagina's "Exchange Value"

Which brings us to another point: the thrill of the chase doesn't just apply to the person who is doing the chasing. Any woman who is the object of a man's desire-driven pursuit knows full well the power she wields. Even feminist Wolf concedes that "a vagina used to have a pretty high 'exchange value,' as Marxist ecomomists would say." Many other aspects of human sexuality favor men, such as a longer reproductive life and socially sanctioned liaisons with women not yet born when they graduated college. So why not at least acknowledge that the timing of lovemaking is one area of dating where you can take control, rather than tacitly accede control to men? And being in control doesn't mean being a "bitch." Bitchiness is synonymous with being mean-spirited, obviously an unattractive attribute in anyone. Exerting control in a relationship means being assertive about what you want, while considering the other person's needs as well.

Women who by virtue of personal or religious values choose to maintain their virginity prior to marriage sometimes understand this principle far better than do their sexually "enlightened" sisters who may be a bit too quick to judge. As research professor Sarah Hinlicky Wilson wrote in a bravely honest blog fifteen years ago, at age twenty-two, "There are so many young women I've known for whom freely chosen sexual activity means a brief moment of pleasure — if that — followed by the unchosen side effects of paralyzing uncertainty, anger at the man involved, and finally a deep self-hatred that is impenetrable by feminist analysis." (Although perhaps perfectly "penetrable" by the economics of emotion, which would contend that the women willingly exchanged sex for, well, nothing.) The present-day version of Wilson's cohorts is the young woman who boasts about her hookups; true to form she sleeps with a cute guy she meets at a party the same night. But the next day, however, she can't stop checking her phone for a text from him that somehow never comes.

The Always-Itch: Testosterone

Imagine that you have an excruciating itch that you have no way of scratching without someone else's help. Now think of the relief that you do feel when that itch is finally scratched. That's precisely what the steroid hormone testosterone does to men, who have twenty times more of it than women. It makes them want to have sex very badly and, depending on their age and overall health, think about and pursue sex near constantly. However, once a guy's testosterone-fueled "itch" is relieved, there's no guarantee that he's going to fall in love with whoever did the scratching. In fact, falling in love actually decreases men's testosterone levels while increasing women's testosterone levels (an effect that promotes pair-bonding). This also means that women tend to get horny once they are having sex in a relationship characterized by secure attachment, in contrast to men, who tend to be at their horniest when *not* in relationships. So for a woman who seeks love from a man, having sex before love shows up is like putting the cart before the horse, biologically at least. In effect, whomever a man turns to the next time he needs his itch scratched depends on many nonbiological factors such as where he is in his life journey, and what he is or isn't looking for in a mate.

Challenges are Hot: Working for It

It's clear that evolutionary forces as well as divergent hormone levels manufactured by the brain's hypothalamus, which is responsible for libido, drive men's and women's fundamentally different approaches to sex. But what both genders do share in common is a typically high degree of satisfaction with something worked hard to obtain, including a sexual encounter.

In a groundbreaking University of Bonn Medical Center study, research subjects who correctly solved math problems were rewarded with money. Functional magnetic brain imaging (fMRI) revealed, however, that people only got excited about monetary rewards when the math problems were difficult. Remarkably, brain scans further revealed that only when the problems were tough did the subjects become distressed when they had to give the money back. Since sex actually "turns on" the same neurons in our brain's reward-responsive nucleus accumbens as does money, it follows that the harder men work to sleep with you, the more gratifying the experience will be. University of Bonn findings can also be extrapolated to suggest that the more challenging it has been for a man to have sex with you, the more he will resist giving it (or you) up.

Equally noteworthy, behavioral psychology persistently demonstrates that the more enjoyable a reward, the more motivated people are to seek out the identical reward again and again. Anyone who has ever gone out of their way to procure a favorite food or repeatedly returned to a favorite vacation spot understands the extraordinary power of such psychological rewards. And a hard-won, hotly anticipated sexual encounter that goes well is about as rewarding as it gets.

Finally, new research reveals that brain levels of dopamine keep rising as we pursue something we want badly. The longer the pursuit, the more dopamine that's released, lending excitement to the chase. Neuroscientists also suggest that when a reward (in this case sex) is delayed, those same dopamine-producing brain cells work even harder to stimulate and promote a stronger drive to attain the goal. Translation: if a man is physically attracted to you but he has to wait for sex, he'll want you even more. That powerful, dopamine-induced drive may also explain, in part, the lure of the unavailable.

Should You Play Hard to Get?

Sleight of hand and twist of fate, on a bed of nails she makes me wait
— Bono

So if we all tend to fall (hard) for what seems unattainable, then shouldn't women play hard to get? Not necessarily. If a man is barely interested in you or not interested at all, then playing hard to get can actually backfire. Notably, you'll mostly be perceived as detached and aloof, essentially unlikeable. This finding comes from a particularly well thought-out experiment conducted by marketing professor Xianchi Di, PhD, and two of his doctorate students at the Chinese University of Hong Kong business school, in which 101 male participants were presented with all sorts of true-to-life dating simulations. The experiment's findings also support more commonly long-held advice; that is, if a man already is at least a little attracted to you, then playing hard to get (e.g., having limited availability to get together, being hard to reach, taking time to return texts/calls, flirting with other men) can, in fact, increase romantic desire and the motivation to chase.

At least at the beginning of a relationship. (Or even in a relationship that's further along but you're feeling taken for granted or underappreciated.) However, know that at some point in an ongoing, established relationship, the dopamine-driven excitement a man experiences from you being unavailable, random, and/or unpredictable will be overshadowed by the satisfaction and fulfillment grounded in your predictability and reliability, essentially trustworthiness. Remember, someone who's *never* rewarded for chasing will eventually stop.

One last note: men get turned on knowing they are dating a woman who's *selectively* hard to get. So if you have been hit on by numerous men in the last few weeks or months but have ignored all but him, do mention that. Conversely, it may be wise to keep to yourself the fact that over the years you have dated/slept with nearly every guy who's asked.

Why We Fall for "Bad Boys"

Interestingly, while men may fall hard for a challenging woman who's just out of his reach, psychological research reveals that we women tend to get turned on by men who are stubborn, self-confident risk takers. According to Gregory Carter of the UK's University of Durham, these men are also charming manipulators with the ability to "sell themselves" to you. And while not necessarily players, the men tend not to make loving, committed partners. So beware, because these oh-so-seductive "bad boys" won't stop chasing — until you're caught. Which is precisely when the meter begins ticking toward the relationship's (short-term) expiration date.

If you can even call what the bad boy offers you a relationship. Consider what happened to cute, vivacious thirty-four year-old Vanessa. Badly scarred from a recent painful breakup with a partner to whom her five-year-old son had become attached, she was gun-shy to jump into anything too intense too soon. That is, until out with friends one evening at an upscale westside bar, Vanessa met Gary, a charming, successful, well-traveled entrepreneur, whom she described as "crazy perfect" — except that he lived across country. After nearly two months of non-stop texting and phone calls, he arranged a trip back out to Los Angeles, answering Vanessa's reluctance to sleep together with: "I'd never, ever hurt you, babe." Of course she believed him.

And true to his word, Gary didn't hurt her — he destroyed her.

Shortly after they had sex, the continual texts, by then joyously integrated into Vanessa's daily life, petered down to next to nothing. Eventually the guy didn't even bother to respond to the reasonable if frustrated texts or calls of, by his own admission, "the most amazing, adorable woman on earth." (Note to all the Ghosting Garys out there: your deafeningly silent disappearance says far more about you than any rough conversation you're avoiding ever could.)

Men's Romantic Side

Taking things slowly also gives romance a better chance; despite common gender stereotyping, men can be just as romantic as women—if not more so. Researchers from Duke University and the University at Albany, SUNY asked 237 state university undergraduates ranging in age from 16 to 25 to hypothetically choose between relationship, career, education, and travel. In addition to rating the importance of these goals, respondents were asked which of the goals they'd sacrifice for romance. Both males and females showed strong desires for individual achievement and intimate relationships. However, defying prediction, men were more likely than women to give priority to a relationship. Specifically, 61 percent of the men chose a romantic relationship over achievement goals, compared to half of the women. Even more telling, nearly a third of male respondents said they'd ditch their education for romance, compared to only 15 percent of females. (That alone proves we're the smarter sex!) Actually, perhaps the men were more reluctant to part with the one peer with whom they feel most comfortable sharing emotional intimacies, whereas women tend to easily open up to one another as well as to their boyfriends. As young men so often describe how they fell deeply in love with the women whom they adore: "She's my best friend—and she's beautiful."

It's not only single undergraduate guys who are highly romantic. For example, married men of all ages tend to give romantic reasons such as, "I knew I couldn't live without her" for choosing a spouse far more often than do their wives, who frequently cite pragmatic factors such as, "I knew he was a great guy who'd make a good husband." (Incidentally, if the women didn't realize that initially, their mothers pointed it out.) Also, when men wait for sex with a particular woman, there's time for a passionate longing or craving to develop. But serve it up too soon, and you'll just provide a forgettable appetizer to the main course your date will inevitably find in someone else, someone for whom he gets so hungry to "taste" that it hurts.

Along these lines, it's noteworthy that of the many online dating anecdotes described in Dan Slater's voluminous *Love in the Time of Algorithms*, the one story that stands out is that of a man who says that he can take things slowly with a pharmacist he's dating and presumably cares for, because there's always someone else to have sex with. As this charmer so eloquently put it, "There is always a pepperoni pizza in the trunk." Point made. (No complicated algorithm needed.)

Also, ladies, you don't have to be a pharmacist or a doctor to warrant a guy's respectful waiting period for your body. Candace, a beautiful exotic dancer, bared it all nearly daily to packed roomfuls of men. Despite describing how she would "put my unit in a guy's face for a better tip," Candace steadfastly maintained her own personal rule of not dating patrons of the strip club where she worked.

Until she met Richard.

Needless to say, Richard was smitten by the curvy performer. He sent Candace weekly bouquets of flowers and even had chicken soup delivered to her dressing room one evening when he noticed her sneezing. Candace somehow resisted Richard's advances for weeks — until one day she didn't. When Candace and Richard saw me for couples therapy (during a particularly rocky patch years later), here's how they described that first hookup: "The sex blew us away." It's doubtful their encounter would have been that powerful had they slept together immediately. Nor would they likely even still be in a relationship. As sociologist Mark Regenerus, PhD, of the University of Texas–Austin writes of early sex: "It's a race to the bottom. Having sex early in a relationship — or, worse, before it even starts — is a guaranteed failure. It's just a matter of time. Men won't sacrifice for someone who's easy. They don't work that way."

The Prospect of Sex Motivates Men to Stick Around

Once you have intercourse with a man, you're taking away a huge inbred incentive for him to get to know you better. Although initially a man may stick around primarily in the hopes of having sex with you, guess what? He often becomes emotionally attached in the meantime. A University of Kansas experiment by psychology professor, Omri Gillath, PhD, using erotic photographs found that "the sheer presence of sexual desire, even when triggered by someone completely unknown, in fact pushes people to do the work of intimacy." Such intimate "work" in the context of a new relationship involves layered self-disclosure as well as lots of day-to-day communication and supportive attention between partners. Furthermore, the simultaneous comfort and excitement reaped from a great physical *and* intellectual/emotional connection increases the likelihood that the relationship will progress to post-sex "stay over" status, versus "after-sex-over-you" dating death. The former trajectory is particularly relevant if you're seeking some form of lasting commitment, or at the very least desire a caring, reciprocal relationship. As a male contributor opined of fast sex in a recent *Los Angeles Times* editorial, "It removes the love, romance, and deep caring from relationships between men and women."

Similarly, don't fool yourself into believing that once a guy has sex with you he's yours. Listen up, ladies: no matter how much he likes it, he's not going to put a ring on it if you give it to him right from the start. Scores of women I've talked to over the years sleep with a guy immediately, mistakenly believing that their irresistible naked bodies and finely honed sexual skills would be enough to stake out a lasting claim on a man, and then they can't understand why he bailed after a few weeks. In fact, the only well-honed intercourse in this scenario is the physical one—the verbal intercourse never had a chance. Because the sex was so readily salient, the men had very little incentive to get to know the women they were sleeping with. And ironically, given these women's misguided beliefs about the power of sex as a stepping-stone to something more, their relationship currency actually became devalued. Renegade actor Charlie Sheen summed up the situation aptly, if unfortunately, in his response to an interviewer who asked him why, as a rich, famous celebrity, he needed to hire prostitutes: "I don't pay for sex; I pay for the women to *leave* in the morning."

Watch Out for His Ego

Even today there are still men whose egos are tied up in playing the traditional male role of sexual aggressor, regardless of background or upbringing. When this role is usurped by their partner, particularly within the early stages of dating, these men feel robbed of their prerogative and control.

One way I've seen this play out is with women immediately proposing a trip with a man she's barely started dating. Yes, there's that double standard again, because guys will often initiate these conversations themselves early on, especially if they're really into a new woman. Nevertheless, two of my male patients became turned off to women they were dating who independently began planning out-of-state trips after only two or three dates; one woman, a movie studio executive, even offered to pay for both their cross-country airline tickets. Once again, the men resented the women's taking the aggressor role, and they also were uncomfortable with the female-initiated fast pacing. Within a few weeks the men did say bon voyage, but it was to the women!

For those who may underrate the power of traditional sexual roles, also known as cultural coding, think about the first question people ask when a baby is born (given no prior sonogram "spoilers"). It's not, "Who does 'it' look like?" but, "Is it a boy or girl?" Our very first socially defining characteristic as we enter the world is based on the anatomical differences between our legs.

Men Who Fall (In Love) Slowly

Just like my trip-declining male patients who never let on to their partners why they were suddenly breaking things off, a slower sexual pace is also preferred by many men who aren't as upfront about it as they could be. So when a new dating partner initiates (hard-core) sex, the men might not refuse what's being offered, but they also don't generally fall in love with the woman. One reason for this is that a faster pace to sex destroys any pleasurable build-up of mystery and eroticism in the relationship; in biochemical terms, the spell-casting neurotransmitter PEA never had time to synthesize. So if you're the one racing into bed, be sure that your date truly is invested in you and is not just going along for the "ride." Otherwise, you'll be setting yourself up for nearly certain disappointment, if not outright heartbreak. Remember: just because you're sleeping with someone doesn't mean you're in a relationship. Likewise, sex won't transform a relationship into something that it's not.

But sometimes simple blind luck will. Notably, in contrast to women who tend to commit to the right guy no matter when she meets him, *timing* is especially critical for men in terms of embarking on a serious relationship. Say you meet a man when many of his peers are marrying, or he decides he wants to start a family, or he's feeling untethered due to the death of a parent or other close family member. Or, regardless of timing, he's simply a stand-up, stand-out, conscientious kind of guy. Then you may expect a somewhat slower sexual pace than if you meet him when he merely wishes to sleep around, no strings attached; some men never even go through that "sow-his-oats" stage at all. As traditional concepts of what constitutes masculinity continue to evolve, men will undoubtedly become more comfortable spontaneously expressing their true attitude toward fast-paced sex, rather than become uninspired participants.

Don't People-Please with Sex

Women of all ages often say yes to things that they don't really want to do to make everyone else happy. This tendency typically traces back to childhood, with girls acculturated to being "people-pleasers." Applied to dating, you may believe that if a guy is spending money on you, you have to have sex with him as a way of paying him back. Not unless you're a hired escort! Joking aside, all you owe a guy who is lavishing money on you is your undivided attention during the date itself. Period. You DO NOT owe him sex.

Among college women in particular, "politeness" currently appears to be overtaking above-described "repay" in dictating sexual consent. As coed Rachel describes in the aforementioned 2018 *New York Times* piece on campus sex and consent: "I hate admitting how much sex I've had because it was 'polite' to just let him finish. You read stories of rape and sexual assault but never about your own manners pressuring you into having sex." Brown University alumna Kat Stoeffel similarly captures the pulse of millennial people-pleasing sex in a 2014 *New York* magazine essay titled, "It Doesn't Have to Be Rape to Suck." She writes: "I know so many women who, late one night, decided it would be rude or un-chill to deny a guy sex after enjoying his company or drinking his alcohol or doing his drugs—or at least not worth the confrontation and social retaliation that could follow." Rude? It's rude to stare at your iPhone when a guy is speaking to you; it's so *not rude* to deny his penis access to your vagina.

Bottom line: save your people-pleasing instincts for agreeing to babysit your neighbor's annoying cat while he's away for the weekend, or wearing that ghastly yellow gown in your college roommate's wedding, but don't people-please by exchanging bodily fluids with men.

Dealing with Pressure to Sleep with You

The flip side to people-pleasing is the guy who attempts to persuade his reluctant acquaintance, friend or date to have sex with him by means of bullying, badgering, taunting, intimidation, guilt-tripping, or manipulation (whew!). Examples include (falsely) promising that sleeping together will strengthen the relationship; or insisting that you must "want it" or you wouldn't have teased/flirted/led him on—even laughed at his jokes. Also, it's unfortunately not uncommon for a guy to insult or ridicule you simply because you've the audacity to turn him down; calling you "uptight" seems to be the putdown of choice these days. (A well-deserved comeback: Dude, get over yourself.) "Standards" means firmly standing your ground. Some of the more pretentious, particularly pushy men will suddenly morph into self-proclaimed shrinks, derisively diagnosing you as having "issues." Don't believe it.

Ever.

You're so much smarter — and stronger — than that. The only "issue" you have is the decree of respecting and standing up for yourself. Which also means that you didn't give in to an entitled guy's perverse power play. Equally disconcerting, men who don't give a hoot about your feelings may simply seize (or orchestrate) a situation where you're particularly vulnerable or your defenses are down. Consider what Caitlin from California recently related to the *New York Times* about a regrettable sexual encounter with a new Tinder match: "At 1 a.m. on a Saturday with a shirtless sophomore, I cared more about how to politely make him leave than standing up for myself." She ended her account with, "But if he hadn't technically done anything wrong, why did I feel so terrible?"

Remember, you don't need a permission slip to skip the sex. If you don't truly want to get naked with him, then don't. Yes, it really is that simple.

Ace Comebacks: When He Tries to Pressure You

<u>Him</u>	<u>You</u>
You're such a tease! You know you want it.	Flirting does *not* mean I want sex.
Let's move this forward already.	The harder you push, the more I pull back.
I'm really falling for you. (He's not.)	That's great, but I don't fall for BS.
You're so uptight/ such a prude.	Dude, get over yourself.
How else can we tell if we're compatible?	That's so lame! Don't even think about it.
Pleeease! I'm begging . . . (Irresistible smile here)	I'm just not ready yet. Give me time.

Emotional Rights and Sexual Boundaries

Although women may have no difficulty establishing a clear physical boundary standing next to a total stranger on an elevator, they appear to have a far tougher time asserting intimate physical boundaries with men they're dating. Certainly, men have a biologically powerful drive for sex, but as previously noted women also have a reproductive right to their partner's support through the lengthy, potentially incapacitating human gestation and nursing periods. Yet even absent an ensuing pregnancy (birth control is superfluous to biology), women's brains still process coitus emotionally. This in stark contrast to men who are hardwired to enjoy sex without any emotional connection.

However, apart from the institution of marriage, society has long since loosened, if not altogether annihilated, sexual boundaries insofar as accommodating the male sexual drive, while completely dismissing women's emotional rights; making it okay for men to sleep with women they don't love or care about. Hence, if you don't establish your own personal boundaries regarding sex, I guarantee that the men you date won't either. (Boundaries intimately involve your body, including how and with whom you wish to share it.) And without any boundaries, you can forget about that enduring "till death do us part" proverbial pact. Although deceptively counterintuitive, when it comes to sex, boundaries actually make things hotter. Unrestrained sex is like a free-for-all junk food binge: it leaves one gluttonously bloated, but ultimately unsatisfied and unfulfilled. Neither men nor women end up enjoying sex as much when there aren't boundaries or restraints in place. Or, as author Shalit states, "[W]hen we humans act like animals without any restraint and any rules, we just don't have as much fun." And of course when there aren't any rules, we are also denied the forbidden fun of *breaking them*.

Breaking Rules: Know When the Time Is Right

Rules to Ignore

Somewhere along the line, almost all sexually active single women ask the same question: "How long do I wait to sleep with a guy I'm dating?" And suddenly everyone they know is an expert, trotting out various sets of "rules." However, when it comes to sleeping with men in today's largely borderless sexual landscape (and please excuse my following momentary lapse into professor-speak) it's important not to be seduced by arbitrary rules that flagrantly disregard crucial gender-based psychosexual precursors and sequelae. In other words, random rules rarely conjure up the science of what makes men and women uniquely want to sleep together and what happens to each of the sexes afterward. To that end, here are a few widely circulated so-called rules to ignore.

First, there's the chauvinistic "three-date" rule that says that if you and your partner aren't having sex by the third date, it's time for him to move on. Assuredly, a woman didn't invent that rule. If a man you're dating still abides by that self-serving, increasingly outdated maxim, then he's likely not someone whom you want to be involved with anyway. The female equivalent to the three-date rule is the "ninety-day" rule, concocted by a dating expert, which pronounces ninety days as the minimum time for a woman to wait before giving it up. (Note: ninety days may be enough time to decide if you want to return a purchased item, but not whether you wish to have sex.) Even if these rules are only meant as guidelines, they are nevertheless counterproductive. They impose baseless, frivolous time limits, to the detriment of suggestible women who are making highly individualized decisions.

Furthermore, even when solid research does inform guidelines, women should still evaluate the results cautiously. For example, psychologist Wendy Walsh, PhD, advocates a thirty-day "love detox" strategy as a test of sorts to determine which men are likely to commit to a woman they're dating. She seems to have fixed upon that number by citing a study that demonstrates that 24 percent of couples who waited thirty days to have sex were still together a year later. Seems promising, right? But think about it: one year later 76 percent, or three out of four of those couples, were *not* together! And thirty days goes by in the blink of an eye; even colleges and universities typically allow more than thirty days for accepted students to commit to their schools. Most men, no matter how commitment-ready and attracted to a particular woman, need longer than the average seventeen-year-old to sign on the dotted line. And so do you.

The Monogamy Conundrum

A better, but nonetheless overly simplistic dating-sex rule invokes monogamy. Today's social norms essentially dictate that a woman sleeps with a man once the relationship is exclusive. It is as though the guy is "paying" for sexual intercourse by sacrificing his freedom to date other women. Therefore, women typically feel obligated to sleep with a man the moment a relationship becomes monogamous. In theory, when the relationship is solid and both people are giving their all, this tradeoff of sorts can work well even without a longer-term commitment. But don't assume that just because a man agrees to be exclusive means that he's falling in love: I've heard far too many guilt-ridden confessions from men who are in monogamous relationships for the "time being," while they simultaneously worry about and plan how they're going to break up with their partner.

And I don't just see these guys in my office. *The Bachelorette* is a reality TV series where a group of approximately twenty-five single men compete for the heart, and hopefully hand in marriage, of one designated bachelorette. In order to be chosen as contestants, the men can't have girlfriends or be involved in relationships. However, in a former episode, an ostensibly serious, back-home girlfriend of one of the contenders ambushed him on air with an angry, tearful tirade where she stated he had "led her on" for a year and a half. According to the girlfriend, his not telling her he was going on a show that focused on "finding love" was clear evidence of his deception. The real clincher was when the guy defended himself by saying that they hadn't been dating each other anymore during his casting call for the show, an assertion the girlfriend vehemently denied. *Yet both he and the woman agreed they had been sleeping together at the time.* So for him — but not his now-ex — at that point sleeping together didn't even signify a dating partnership. Oops.

The male *Bachelorette* contestant described above most likely falls into the category of pathological liar, or at least pathological something. Even so, if you find yourself sleeping with man after man in a series of monogamous, but ultimately disappointing, relationships, it might be time to reassess your own benchmarks for sexual intimacy, as well as your dating-sexual style. (See Appendix 3)

When You Can't Decide

Coming full circle from the starting point of self-respect high-lighted in Step 1, if and when you sleep with someone will depend largely on your own well-informed choice, as well as on the intricacies of each individual relationship. Departing from today's self-imposed arbiters of sexual norms, Step 9 demonstrates that "manufactured" parameters such as number of dates, passage of time, or exclusivity in a relationship oversimplify a highly private, complex decision. Essentially, the primary rule you should be following as to when to have sex is the rule of your head and your heart. Your own judgment and instincts won't lead you astray; other people's mostly contrived standards will.

As a woman of today you personally may or may not need love, or any other justification for sleeping with a man. But infinite hours of testimony from both women and men do highlight ten useful guidelines in order to better enjoy the experience and avoid feeling used or resentful afterward, whether in or out of a relationship. The checklist is also especially helpful for times that you may be confused or unsure.

How to Decide: The Best "Yes"

1. Self-esteem and self-respect
2. Autonomous decision
3. Trust in your partner
4. Mutual respect
5. Mutual attraction
6. Consistent affection/attention
7. Sustained comfort in partner's presence
8. Empathy/compassion (Partner demonstrates empathy for you.)
9. Value (Partner highly values you.)
10. Emotional intimacy (Sharing of confidences; mutual support)

The first item on the list is arguably the most important in that a threshold level of self-esteem and self-respect prevents women, especially young women, from engaging in sex (particularly oral sex) out of obligation, need for attention, or just because everyone else *seems* to be doing it. In fact, it's critical that women don't devalue themselves in any realm, whether sexual, professional, or otherwise. And autonomy, which is defined here as independently assuming responsibility for one's own decisions and actions, is equally imperative. In other words, don't blame your partner if you have regrets: the bed you make is yours alone to lie in — especially afterward. A strong sense of autonomy also helps preempt peer pressure as well as coercive sex. Clearly, self-esteem, self-respect, and autonomous decision making render the sex psychologically sound, whether or not there is the hope or expectation of continuing a relationship with one's partner. Which means you may be open to the possibility of casual sex purely for pleasure, curiosity, or "just because" but at the very least don't want to feel seedy or violated during or afterwards. The addition of items 3 through 7 (mutual trust, respect, attraction, affection, as well as a high degree of comfort in your partner's presence) set the stage for more intense romance: that's typically when sleeping with a guy "feels" incredibly right as the relationship progresses.

If you do desire a long-term commitment, then interpersonal attributes 8, 9, and 10 take on added importance. For example, the psychological trait of empathy (number 8) is often overlooked by women when they're soul mate shopping, but can make or break a relationship. Even the word "empathy" itself derives from the Greek term for passion and physical affection. Notably, before sleeping with a man it is preferable that he has demonstrated empathy and compassion for you in various situations. If not, you may be headed for a cruel awakening in the bedroom, which provides a litmus test of a man's empathy and basic human decency (or lack thereof). Think about it: Do you want to undress a man's true personality when he is lying on top of you naked and panting, or do you want to know his naked truths before the two of you are undressed? Interestingly, as a side note, research has demonstrated empathy, along with self-esteem and autonomy, to be characteristic of the best lovers of both sexes. And list items 9 and 10 (your value to your partner and emotional intimacy) are crucial to the development of long-term commitment. If both are absent, it doesn't matter if you're a Miss Universe with porn-star skills — the relationship is going nowhere. That is, nowhere but the bedroom.

What's Love Got to Do with It?

Despite frequent one-nighters — and sometimes even because of them — many women eventually find themselves yearning for a partner that loves and treats them well. Not that the occasional hookup or two, depending on circumstances, can't be empowering. But hands down, over time women will say sex in a relationship beats casual sex. In a related vein, women especially covet a love confession that accompanies or immediately follows intercourse. Interestingly, a 2011 survey of 84 female and 35 male undergraduates at a southwestern university found that when given a choice in a hypothetical romantic relationship where they hadn't yet been "sexually intimate" with their partner, the women preferred a post-sex to a pre-sex profession of love. (The men, however, preferred a hypothetical partner's pre-sex love profession, presumably because it indicated they'd soon get laid.) Hypotheticals notwithstanding, I believe women actually want to hear a (genuine) "I love you" sometime pre *and* post intercourse. Perhaps that's because not only is it indescribably reassuring to know you are truly loved by the person with whom you are about to share the most physically intimate act of human life, but as the researchers noted, women realize a man's post-sex love confession typically comes with a commitment.

Love in this context — that is, in an attached, secure relationship — brings that wonderfully complex "3-D" perspective of desire, dedication, and deep caring. It's all about mutual support and attention melded with sharing and passion. Also, women nearly unanimously express how "safe" they feel in a great relationship where a partner has their back. Here, sexual intercourse is the super sweet spot that tends to affirm love, not force it. Nevertheless, as an experienced clinician, I also know that love can very well develop some time after sex, and many relationships do, in fact, follow that trajectory. Given the sexual smorgasbord available to men these days, however, for a serious post-sex progression you must at the very least ensure beforehand that you're not merely another throwaway bagel. Otherwise you're just rolling the dice.

He Loves Me . . . He Loves Me Not

Consider twenty-six-year-old Olivia's experience with a guy she'd been seeing exclusively for nearly a year. Granted, her partner's rigorous joint business/law school curriculum didn't leave much free time, but somehow he managed to hang with his buddies every Saturday night — without her. When Olivia complained, he consoled her with, "You know I love you." And then there were all those times he declined sex (she even invested in new lingerie) because he said he was preparing for some exam or other. This bright medical student assuaged her disappointment for months by reminding herself of her boyfriend's heavy workload — until one evening she noticed that all he actually seemed to be studying was online porn.

Regardless of whether you've been together for a while — or barely at all — a man's actions and even mannerisms toward you are just as telling as his words, if not more so. Olivia herself remarked that she would have ditched this guy sooner, sparing herself "wasted aggravation and the eight pounds I gained on account of that pathetic perv douchebag," had she paid closer attention to the following questions:

- Does your guy want to spend as much time with you as possible?
- Do you ever "catch" him smiling or gazing at you adoringly?
- Is he attentive/passionate/devoted? (Any one of these is fine.)

- Does he put effort into the relationship?
- Do you laugh together easily and often?
- Does he try hard to "win you back" if you have a fight or temporarily separate?
- Does he put his own needs or wishes secondary to yours at least some of the time?
- Does he overlook your more annoying idiosyncrasies?
- Has he ever been excited to give you a thoughtful gift or to do something special that he knows is meaningful to you?
- If needed, would he be willing to help you out financially or with a significant commitment of time or energy?
- Does he want to meet your friends and/or family?

Regarding the last question above, if someone you're involved with is motivated to get together with your friends and family, and tries to make an especially good impression when he does, that's generally a strong sign of dedication to you. Which means that presuming you feel the same about him, there could be a future. In contrast, a man who avoids a woman's family, especially without provocation, typically isn't in the relationship for the long haul and thus doesn't want to engage in a deceptive charade. Also, he may just be experiencing the slightest bit of guilt if he's leading you on, which is another reason he doesn't want to be paraded before your relatives.

The fact is that there is a very fine line between leading a woman on and flat-out lying. Not surprisingly, the late psychologist Dory Hollander, PhD, author of *101 Lies Men Tell Women — and Why Women Believe Them* found the most prevalent lie among men is claiming to love a woman in order to manipulate her into bed. Case in point: Ziba, a twenty-five-year-old virgin, described how excited and happy she was when a guy she'd just started dating a few weeks back told her he loved her. However, when she made it clear she wasn't ready to sleep with him, her boyfriend-hopeful had his friend (who happened to be her brother) break the news to Ziba that he didn't want to see her anymore. Love? Yeah, right.

Ziba's experience notwithstanding, I'd surmise that the "I love you" lie has long since been dethroned. Specifically, men no longer need to tell women they love them in exchange for sex because so many women today eagerly oblige without love. Nevertheless, there's a very good chance that somewhere down life's unpredictable path, even the most stalwart love-skeptic may find herself unexpectedly longing for *l'amour* — and to hear *je t'adore*.

Nevertheless, if you haven't yet heard the ever-magic three words "I love you" — in any language — or you're not feeling loved or treasured in a relationship, sex is typically not going to get you there. And the only soul mate in your near future may be the one in your shoes. In your next relationship, therefore, it may be wise to strive for a firmly established bond, along with some evidence that you're highly valued by a man, before sleeping with him, particularly if you seek a long-term commitment. Try focusing on pulling the guy up psychologically rather than pulling down his pants. Remember, we value those who make us feel good about ourselves. The same goes for you letting a guy in: take risks, open up, be vulnerable. At its best, emotional intimacy opens up our vulnerabilities and involves caring for, confiding in, and trusting each other not despite, but *with*, our flaws. You'll realize a much more profound connection — with a better chance of genuine love — than when the sex comes first.

Finally, returning to the issue of monogamy, if a guy you're really into is seeing other people while he's sleeping with you, forget about that long-term commitment; he isn't even committing to the short term! That said, exclusivity alone doesn't ensure commitment, but if you're exclusive in a relationship that checks most of the Best "Yes" boxes, then you have a very good shot at that (hopefully happy) ever after with your man. *At last.*

Step 9 Playlist ♫
With or Without You/U2
Single Ladies/Beyoncé
What's Love Got to Do with It/Tina Turner
At Last/Etta James

And she was hot, as she kissed my mouth
And she was hot, as I wiped her brow

—Mick Jagger

Step 10

Bring It: Best. Sex. Ever. (*Your* Choice)

Pick up nearly any popular women's magazine today and you'll see a boldfaced version of the following: "Men want sex, but women want good sex." The problem is that unlike men, women apparently aren't getting what they want. To wit, while more and more single young women are engaging in lots of sex, self-report surveys show that they aren't enjoying it. Consider the following: in a 2011 nationwide study of 3,237 young adults aged nineteen to twenty-five, 90 percent of men experienced orgasm "most or all of the time," while that figure dropped to 47 percent for women. Also, of this same sample, only 37 percent of women claimed to "very much" enjoy giving oral sex, compared with 67 percent of already significantly smaller numbers of male, um, oral participants (on the giving end). Meaning that, in plain speak, although fewer numbers of men go down on women than vice versa, most of the ones who do actually enjoy it compared to female "givers." (The researchers explained their use of orgasm and oral sex as criteria of sexual satisfaction, noting that these components are highly valued in American culture—for better or worse.)

The point is that you're just not having as much fun during sex as guys are. And no matter how many (excuse my crudeness) blow jobs you're giving during casual hookups, your partners likely aren't pleasuring you. This supposition is consistent with the Online College Social Life Survey's finding that during hookups women were much more likely to give men oral sex than to receive it. Furthermore, according to the study, "Women seem to believe that they're supposed to be pleasing in both hookups and relationships." However, as lead researcher Dr. Paula England concluded, "Guys don't seem to care as much about women's pleasure in the hookup, whereas they do seem to care quite a bit in relationships." This finding corroborates informal online surveys in which men say that they try hard to please sexually in relationships because they want to keep you close to them and away from other men. They genuinely care about you and your pleasure, and your perception of their bedroom skills means a lot to them. Not so in (very) casual hookups where a man's immediate sexual gratification typically trumps his regard for the woman. Nor will it bother hookup-guy if you subsequently get together with someone else, because he doesn't care enough about you to be jealous.

It's also not just large numbers of young women who don't appear to be enjoying sex much these days. An Australian survey of unmarried women aged forty-five to fifty-nine in relationships found that only 51 percent experienced "physical pleasure," although limited frequency of sex also factored into their dissatisfaction.

In addition to the predominant focus on *his* pleasure during casual sex, I've observed another common behavioral pattern among women that may explain those let's-get-it-over-with encounters. Namely, women with limited enjoyment of sex are focusing too heavily on technique and what they feel they "should" be doing in bed to please their partner and not enough on the sensuality of the experience itself. Sensuality provides the soundtrack to sex in much the same way a musical score provides the soundtrack to a movie: if it were absent, the "job" would still get done — it just wouldn't be nearly as pleasurable or memorable. And when you listen to great, pleasing music, your brain doesn't attempt to pick apart and analyze the instrumentation; it just loves what it hears. The same goes for sex, dear reader. *Go for the WOW, not the how.* Sensually focused sex makes that possible.

Get Down for Sensually Focused SEX

Sensually focused sexual activity has three simple, basic components: **S**avor, **E**xplore, and **"X"**cite. (Thus, the acronym "SEX.") The "Savor" component of SEX amplifies anticipatory eroticism; the "Explore" component tunes you into touch and sensation; and "X"cite (excite) shows how to sustain a partner's lust for you and keep the sex fresh and exciting. Savor and Explore are loosely based on the early work of pioneering sex therapy researchers William Masters and Virginia Johnson, but with several important differences. For example, while Masters and Johnson emphasize the verbal communication of needs from first kiss forward, SEX discourages such cerebral, nonphysical communication when a couple has just begun having sex. In other words, dial down the dialog and enjoy the passion of the moment. This modification is consistent with new research indicating that mindfulness enhances sexual pleasure, and conversation during sex is not conducive to mindfulness. Sure, it's okay to briefly mention what you are feeling right then and there, but much more than that will mostly distract you from your own sensations. Communication takes many forms. Punctuating your encounter with brief verbal comments and cues is fine, just as long as they don't escalate into a "tutorial" of sorts. Also, if you try to talk less, you'll be pleasantly surprised at how much you really can "say" physically. Unspoken sexual communication can be just as powerful, if not more so, than words in bed. (And of course there's always the conversational postmortem anytime, anyplace afterward.)

SEX also brings out the playful and adventuresome Aphrodite in you: first, through intimate, erotic exploration of each other's *entire* body and, later, by the infusion of novelty and risk into sexual encounters. Plus, guess what men say is the number-one turn-on for them in bed? Being with an adventurous woman! Which brings us back to those headlines: yes, women do want really good sex, but guys actually do, too. And judging by the already overriding positive feedback, you're *both* going to be getting it with SEX.

10 Things to Do to Ensure Good Sex

- Dial down the dialogue; amp up unspoken, physical communication.
- Shut out all distractions, especially those in your head.
- Look your partner directly in the eyes — and keep looking.
- Tease when taking off clothes: yours or his.
- Take a few belly, burlesque, pole or jazz-funk dance classes.
- Enjoy your nakedness by banishing thoughts of bodily imperfections.
- Be adventurous; let yourself go.
- Explore his entire body, not just his genitals.
- Engage all your senses (listen to sounds, take in scents).
- Praise your partner's efforts (makes him want to please you more).

SAVOR Sensual Moments

The beginning of a sexual relationship with a new partner can be exciting and stressful all at once. Notably, no matter how aroused they are, some women find it difficult to be fully present sexually. The key here is to shut out all distractions, especially any mental self-talk such as potential insecurity about your body or the relationship. (Trust me, there'll be plenty of time later to mull things over. Don't spoil the moment by doing it now.) Likewise, don't be an "observer" watching or censoring yourself or, equally bad, your partner. Now isn't the time for judgment; in fact, the noisy part of your brain needs to be set to silent. This takes considerable practice, including during other focused, nonsexual times, but it's doable. The more adept you are at letting go of extraneous thoughts, the more pleasure you'll derive from savoring exclusively sensual stimuli as they unfold.

Begin by letting your eyes do the talking. Warm, engaged sensual eye contact results in the immediate release of pleasurably exciting brain neurotransmitters in the same manner as discussed in the "The Look" section on flirting (Step 7). Also, don't just run into the bathroom and undress; you are about to make love to a trusted mate, not undergo a physical exam. For instance, tease him as you take off your clothes, and the ensuing lusty tension between you two will be palpable. (On an interesting, counterintuitive side note, one of my patients who had a brief stint as a camgirl described the "powerful" feeling she got from stripping for fully clothed men.) Similarly, if you really want to go all out, take a few belly, burlesque, or pole dancing classes. It's not just for your "audience"; these are all dance forms that get women in touch with their own sexuality. You'll get so turned on discovering moves you didn't even know your body could make that you'll hardly be able to wait to get into bed with your lucky partner. More mainstream, contemporary dance styles like jazz-funk, which involves lots of booty action (think: Brittany Spears or Beyoncé), also do the trick. Overall, as you let go of inhibitions and *own yourself,* your body becomes fierce, powerful, smoking hot—even if pre-dance you'd have felt it's not.

If dance (or striptease) just isn't your thing, no matter. Simple actions like taking off your sweater or top in a single cross-armed over-the-head motion have been shown to excite men sexually even if you're fully clothed underneath. (This is because of conditioning: men have frequently been rewarded with "pleasurable sights" at the end of similar motion sequences by women.) But when you finally do take it all off, if your modesty and/or non-swimsuit-issue-type body still compel you to hide naked under the covers, don't worry. Many men describe your em-barr-assed, bare-ass shyness as an endearing turn-on. To turn up the heat, however, you might try painstakingly undressing your man, for example button by button on his shirt. Then, just before the last button, place your parted lips on your partner's neck or belly for a moment, and watch as his sexual arousal (ahem) soars. Have fun experimenting and developing your own sensual MO, then run with it instead of with the former running commentary in your head.

Assuming you've followed the signature message of *Don't Sleep with Him Yet*, it will be much easier to confidently banish intrusive thoughts because you know that your partner has hung around for *you* — not just for sex. It also may help to realize, ladies, that once they actually are having sex, men tend to be far more forgiving about your body than you are yourself. So while you may be wasting precious present moments worrying about a few spots of cellulite, your partner's heady arousal is blinding him to your self-perceived physical imperfections. Put in simpler terms, once they have you naked, men don't care. (With the exception of players, who do.) Now is the time to truly just let yourself go. Your brain is already fired up by dopamine and phenethylamine (PEA), chemical neurotransmitters that surge with sexual excitement, and your body responds in kind. But it's ultimately up to you to be completely in the here and now in order to fully savor the steamy eroticism of the encounter. This takes a fair amount of practice; however, the results are worth it. You eventually will be far more tuned in to the dopamine-blasting, life-affirming high of sex.

EXPLORE Each Other's Bodies

Even animals experience phenomenal pleasure and orgasms when it comes to mating. But what differentiates people from animals is that for us sex isn't all about procreation. That's the reason why "making love" is a far more popular term than "copulating" when referring to human intercourse. On a side note, words and language can be as much a form of sexual foreplay as are intimate kisses and touching — especially outside of bed. What does *not* constitute sexy foreplay, however, is groping. (Read: bumbling and/or creepy guys who try to cop a feel.) Paradoxically, women often complain about a lack of foreplay, yet they also frequently get grabby for a guy's genitals while neglecting the rest of his body. Hence the "E" in SEX, which stands for "Explore" using *all* your senses. The antithesis of merely "screwing," Explore emphasizes deliberate, sensual entire-body focus as a vital element of sex.

Every couple has their own sexual rhythm, so to speak, and every sexual encounter is slightly different, even between the same two people. But whether you're swept off your feet by a peacocky show of prowess, or whether it's his seductively subtle moves that melt you, exploring each other's bodies takes the intimacy even further. Young children do this innocently and naturally; there is an inherent joy in exploring an opposite-sex body. This form of exploration is not about sexual "technique" or skill, which often comes off as mechanical and contrived, particularly in the early stages of sexual bonding. Rather, the focus is on spontaneity and, once again, letting yourself go. Massaging your guy's feet, lightly tickling (or licking) his legs, running your fingers through his hair, stroking his face, and listening to his pounding heart constitute erogenous exploration that ironically sometimes comes off even more intimately than touching and tasting his genitals.

As emphasized, physical exploration is equated with a full-on *sensual* experience as much as a sexual one. For example, most women are aware of how sensual and erotic French kissing can be, but they unfortunately tend to lose that sensual focus somewhere along the road to harder-core sex. In a similar vein, a man's genitals are comprised of much more than just his penis. You know that song by John Mayer, "Your Body Is a Wonderland"? (A self-professed stud; he should know.) Well, so is your man's body, and if you approach it as such you'll be likelier to appreciate its masculine sensuality — assuming that you're with somebody you really want to be with. Otherwise, fellatio, literally "to suck" in Latin, will suck indeed when treated as a must-do, expedient act to "get over with." Conversely, even "caveman" primal sexual sounds like grunts, groans, and moans can be a turn-on for you with the right man. Note that unlike men, who become excited by seeing a naked female body, women become turned on predominantly by how they *feel* about their man. Surprisingly, the six-pack abs and toned buttocks that do it for you the rest of the time become far less relevant in bed. But that mischievous smile of his works its magic always.

Note that at some point you'll undoubtedly want to ask your guy what feels best and what he likes. (And vice versa.) But contrary to what your overdriven, analytic brain is accustomed to, if you start asking too many questions too soon, you run the risk of dampening the early passion by emphasizing the "how" rather than the "WOW." Also, unless you're involved with a sexual novice or one of the 33 percent of men who apparently don't enjoy giving oral sex, your sexy exploration of your bae's body will likely serve as a model for him to reciprocate with a pleasure tour of his own. (To wit: "I could drink a case of you, darling.") And you know how remarkably spine tingling this can feel. Truly, as the brain relays X-rated messages to and from excited nerve endings, one often experiences internal "shivers" of pleasure, a precursor to orgasm. In fact, a guy who is genuinely into you (figuratively, that is) will move mountains to please you; in bed all he has to "move" is you.

Women who are adored by their boyfriends understand that a good degree of a man's self-esteem is wrapped up in how he views himself as a lover. So no matter who happens to be doing the touching and tasting—hopefully this will all be intertwined at some point—please let your partner know how aroused you become when he also explores your body sensually apart from intercourse. An added benefit (in addition to making your guy feel like Superman) is that complimenting him on his noncoital, amorous skills will relieve him of a great deal of performance anxiety that almost all men experience at least sometimes. What's more, a caring guy who is no longer preoccupied in bed with how he measures up will become a far more sexually empathic and present partner. The icing on the cake: increased trust and cherishing of one another that follows.

Having come this far, it's time for some practice! See Appendix 4 for a SEX-based exercise that you can use with your partner as a seductive prelude to intercourse or as a sexy activity on its own.

"X"CITE with Hot, Edgy Sex

---

10 Ways to Keep the Sex Going Strong

- Infuse novelty into encounters (not just the bedroom).
- Do sexy stuff together (steamy shower, skinny dipping).
- Take vacations to rekindle spark.
- Add element of surprise (naked under trench coat).
- Vary sex "prequel."
- Add thrill of risk (make out in public).
- Send sexy texts/notes.
- Have sex after adrenaline-rush activities (roller coaster, scary movie).
- Engage all senses (auditory/music; gustatory/syrups; olfactory/scents).
- Utilize fantasy scenarios.

When you're infatuated with a man, and he with you, the excitement will take care of itself. In addition to dopamine and norepinephrine, both of your brains will be flooded with the amphetamine-like neurotransmitter phenethylamine (PEA), lending a "charged-up," thrilling, exhilarating feeling to sex. However, although hopefully your partner will stick around longer than eighteen months, PEA doesn't. The consensus among scientists is that the chemical gradually dissipates from eighteen months to three years into a relationship. (Nature figured you'd be pregnant by then.) At this point the attachment or "cuddle chemical" oxytocin takes over inasmuch as it is no longer overshadowed by PEA.

Oxytocin is an endorphin that renders a sense of security, and it is released by the pituitary gland in both women and men during sexual contact, or even during a 20-second hug. Oxytocin, which promotes pair-bonding in humans, is to attachment what PEA is to arousal. Getting physical generates those positive, immensely comforting feelings that makes us want to stay with the person the feelings are associated with. So the good news is that thanks to oxytocin, you and a beloved sexual partner already are feeling very attached to one another, which nature intended so you'd stay together to raise your offspring. Oxytocin also motivates couples to stick together through the "for worse" phases of their relationship. PEA is hotter-than-hell-happiness (think: racing stallion—Or Porsche convertible); oxytocin is forever-cozy (think: cuddly teddy bear—or any car with seat heaters.)

The problem is that there will inevitably come a day when just a sexy little glance from you doesn't trigger his dopamine like it once did. And with the brain's own love drug—that is, PEA—gradually diminishing in both sexes, instead of physiological neurotransmitters automatically perpetuating the sexual Nirvana, sustaining the heat with a long-term partner increasingly becomes up to you. But there's no need to panic that your guy will be on the prowl because he misses the heady high provided by a new partner (unless of course you happen to be dating Tiger Woods). Decades of reliable research has revealed other factors besides brain chemistry that greatly contribute to sexual excitement.

First and foremost, studies have consistently shown that both novelty as well as risk can significantly increase sexual arousal. With regard to novelty, one way to keep it hot is by having sex in different, new places. Vacation spots are known to work well because of their obvious novelty factor; however, so do easily overlooked but omnipresent places like in front of the full-length mirror in your bathroom. (Placing a beach towel down first helps avoid floor burns.) Additionally, speaking of bathrooms, start your day once in a while with a *surprise* full-steamy joint shower—your guy will be distracted all day long by even steamier thoughts of you. In fact, research demonstrates that novel stimuli, which have the added element of being unique or unexpected, are especially effective at intensifying sexual desire—so showing up at his place at an opportune time with nothing on under your trench coat is more than just a classic movie cliché.

And ladies, along these same lines, do vary the sex prequel once in a while; for example, if you typically have sex after an evening out (or cozy evening in), surprise your guy one morning with seductive touches and moves under the sheets. Even better, tease him under those too-small tables at coffee houses, because now you've added the vital element of *risk* in being seen. But please use discretion: while you may not mind being thrown out of Coffee Bean, you probably wouldn't want to be escorted off a plane! Similarly, note that you don't have to do it in Central Park (an extreme example of indiscretion) to add the thrill of risk to your partnering — even enjoying a heart-racing activity together like a super scary ride at an amusement park will lend intensity to the afterward-sex.

Additionally, don't overlook the small risks. For example, sending your man a sexy text when you *know* he's in the middle of a business meeting, telling him what you plan on doing to him after work will put the kind of smile on his face that will make others enviously wonder what he just read. Even better, your unexpected, racy note will have him counting the hours until he sees you. A word of caution, however: don't try this, my friend, when you first begin dating someone. It will backfire as a turnoff rather than a turn-on, and you'll be viewed less as good-crazy versus just plain nutcase-crazy.

Similarly, if you really want to have some fun, watch how excited that guy you've been seeing — and doing — becomes when, out of the blue at a party, you playfully whisper in his ear that you want to "lick, taste, kiss, and suck" him (all sensually focused acts, by the way). Or if that's too much, seductively whispering "Let's get out of here" has the same effect. And about that "lick," add another flavorful dimension to the most specialized sense in the body, that of taste: champagne, Grand Marnier, whipped cream, flavored brandy, even chocolate or raspberry syrup all go scrumptiously with skin. Similarly, discover how completely different an erotic massage can feel when performed by the same person just by varying the fragrant oils used. (Try patchouli, vanilla, or mandarin orange—all associated with sexual attraction—for starters.) Or how various scented candles affect mood and ambience. (Pumpkin pie and cinnamon, for example, have been demonstrated to increase arousal in both genders; experts attribute this effect to their homey, cozy vibe.) All sorts of sensual stimuli can suddenly turn us on anew, from your lingering perfume (or his aftershave) right down to the scent of home-baked bread.

Our senses, although powerfully erotic, are essentially grounded in reality. Yet another more imagination-reliant way to change up your same old sex scene—quite literally—is through fantasy. It is perhaps sadly telling that the most common fantasy among married couples (cited by researchers) is sex with a different partner. However, in your dating relationship, being creative and playful with varied role-playing, at least once in a while, can keep things remarkably new and fresh, even with the same person. For example, Kathryn, a urologist, described how surprisingly turned on both she and her long-term boyfriend became from just a very brief moment of foreplay fantasy involving doctors and patients. And if you're one of the approximately 125 million women worldwide who own a copy of the erotic novel *Fifty Shades of Grey*, then you already have a roadmap to soft-core BDSM (bondage/submission/sadism/masochism) on your bedside. Men apparently share your kinky pleasure: 39 percent of both married men and men in consensual sexual relationships have domination fantasies, according to international sex researcher Claude Crépault. Okay, this may be getting a bit carried away, dear reader, but what is sex for if not to be transported to another dimension by someone you find pretty out of this world, too?

In summary, SEX is about much more than your guy just wanting it; you had that from the start. And it's not about him groveling (although granted, that doesn't hurt either). Rather, SEX lends a whole new meaning to being "good in bed," because with its sensual focus you truly experience each other as never before. Likewise, you won't ever again take for granted your own extraordinary female body and its luscious sensuality. Sex may have made its entrance later in the pages of this book — and in some of your own stories — but you'll be blown away by how much better it is than anything you could have imagined. And *that* surely is worth the wait.

Step 10 Playlist ♫
She Was Hot/Rolling Stones
Your Body Is a Wonderland/John Mayer
A Case of You/Joni Mitchell

Just for Fun:

EMPOWERING EXTRAS

The essence of life is the smile of round female bottoms, under the shadow of cosmic boredom.

—Guy de Maupassant

Hot Stuff:

From Plain to Pretty, and Pretty to Drop-Dead Gorgeous

*A*ppearance matters. It's really as simple as that. Sure, there are lots of other forms of human capital besides looks — intelligence, sense of humor, and kindness to name a few — but appearance is, and always will be, an extremely valuable bartering chip for women in the romantic realm. Nevertheless, there are many well-intentioned therapists who indiscriminately impart the tired platitude that what's on the inside is what counts. That is, of course, true overall, but there are times when a woman may need a far more banal mirror to reflect on how to attract men. Although most men eventually realize that "inside" qualities such as character and attitude make up the mortar of relationships, their initial approach is frequently in the direction of a pretty girl.

But don't despair because, like most of us, you often avoid mirrors altogether. (Fluorescent-lit ones in ladies' rooms are especially bad.) There are many very easy — even fun — "fixes" that will nonetheless make a huge difference in your appearance and confidence. Also, a surprising added benefit to enhancing your appearance is that, as this bonus section demonstrates, your physical health, mood, and even mental sharpness may significantly improve as well. And that's anything but shallow.

"Mirror, Mirror . . ." Men Don't Play Fair

I admit that I judge books by their covers. Well, maybe I don't actually judge them, but I've certainly bought more than a few books because I liked their covers and hoped that the contents wouldn't disappoint. Applied to dating, given no prior interaction (including flirtatious signals), a new man you meet will primarily be attracted by your looks.

One of the first research studies to systematically investigate this intuitive fact was a now-classic psychosocial study conducted at the University of Minnesota. The study found that when men were introduced to random women at a party or other social event, and then given surveys to complete, the single best predictor of whether a man wanted to see a woman again was her physical attractiveness. Even high intelligence and exceptional social skills couldn't match it. (Lest you believe college-aged men's brains have changed much, consider how Tinder's extraordinary appeal to young men rests primarily on *pictures* of women.)

Similarly, in another compelling research study conducted in 2005, University of Pennsylvania psychologists surveyed participants of HurryDate, a three-minute speed dating service, about how they chose their dates. Once again, men relied mainly on physical attractiveness, largely disregarding factors such as profession and personality. As the study authors so aptly noted, the men were given three minutes to choose their dates, but they could have made the same choices in three seconds. This observation also corroborates the provocative theme of author Malcolm Gladwell's popular book *Blink*, which proposes that upon first meeting, people make immediate, lasting judgments about one another in less time than it takes to blink. And that's not nearly enough time to size up your beautiful spirit.

Economist Daniel Hamermesh stretches the initial powerful advantage beauty bestows early on in the dating game even further by arguing that whether it's higher pay at work — or a higher-earning spouse — more attractive women (and men) fare better. In *Beauty Pays: Why Attractive People Are More Successful*, he writes, "Most generally, beauty will be associated with any characteristic that brings more to the partnership, including the partner's ability to provide material things — his or her ability to earn money." Lest you feel completely disillusioned at this point, please note that Hamermesh does mention mitigating "advantageous" attributes, such as "intelligence, height, sex appeal, family name, or whatever," that someone can offer to a potential spouse in place of looks. (Incidentally, I believe the category of "whatever" yields infinite possibilities.) Nevertheless, the University of Texas–Austin-based author cites credible research (including additional speed dating studies) in conjunction with economic theory to support his primary contention that "beauty matters more to men, and potential economic success matters more to women's dating choices."

Science further buttresses behavioral studies by revealing that men are far more visual than women and will first be drawn to a potential mate by her appearance. There is an evolutionary basis to this phenomenon: men prefer to mate with women with symmetrical features and big, alert eyes that signify health and fertility. But even if you and your potential partner aren't planning on propagating the human species, it really helps move things forward if your appearance holds at least some appeal. Which brings us to those unfair slights (granted, by the "wrong" guys) that often start early and sometimes continue for decades. Yes, that cute guy in your chemistry lab whom you let cheat off you — all semester — should have invited you to his party. (Your grungy sweats — all semester — notwithstanding.) Yes, that divorced, dimpled accountant you were chatting up at the fundraiser should have asked for your number. (Despite the "as-is" no-makeup-but-needs-it look.) Then again, who said that life or, more specifically, men are fair?

That said, you don't have to look like Megan Fox or Halle Berry (who, by the way, have both expressed genuine insecurities about their looks) to get a guy to notice you and ask you out. Know that just by virtue of being female you are, as Christina Aguilera's timeless lyrics proclaim, beautiful. My added spin: it's badass to own your unique appearance, blemishes and all, but accepting things doesn't mean you stop trying. Beauty and brains aren't mutually exclusive, or as actress Cate Blanchett put it, "Being attractive does not preclude being intelligent." This was in response to a journalist at the 2018 Cannes Film Festival (where she was jury president) who asked how female empowerment squares with gowns and high heels. I'd add that feeling attractive can actually be highly empowering in and of itself. As a corollary, instead of wasting so much mental energy doubting yourself (which we all can't help at times), try making the most of what you have. For example, Kim Kardashian's derriere and even Michelle Obama's muscular arms are defining features of their own beauty that don't fit typical standards. And consider that Gwyneth Paltrow was voted World's Most Beautiful Woman by *People* magazine in 2013 at the age of forty. She has a great smile—and masterfully packages her blonde, fresh-faced (but not striking) looks. Gwyneth also knows the value of exercise—lots and lots of it.

Why We Gain Weight with Age (And How to Prevent It)

Although Gwyneth's daily, two-hour, trainer-monitored workouts may not exactly fit the frazzled plebian lifestyle of most of us non-Hollywood goddesses, I wholeheartedly agree with her admission that "exercise helps me feel my best." And if that isn't enough to get your booty moving, consider this: according to the American Medical Association, the average weight gained by Americans between the ages of twenty-five and fifty-five is one and a half pounds per year!

Surprisingly, bioresearch has shown that this weight gain is not due to the mere process of aging, but rather because we tend to be less physically active as we get older. The American College of Sports Medicine recommends a minimum of 150 minutes per week of exercise for weight control. Doing the math, that works out to two and one-half hours of exercise weekly, distributed any way you choose. Even thirty minutes of brisk walking five days a week counts.

Remember: you don't have to be thin to look good. Many larger-framed women whose bodies aren't meant to be skinny can easily handle some weight and still look great; also, sex appeal is body shape non-discriminatory. But if your favorite jeans won't zip up, it may be time to lose the excuses—and the extra pounds.

Get Moving! (Hotter, Happier, and Healthier)

While regular cardio exercise is exemplary, it's simply not going to happen given many superwomen's super-packed lives dominated by time stress, which is what we experience when it feels like there aren't enough hours in a day to "get it all done." Unless, that is, you find a form of exercise that you truly look forward to and miss if you don't do. You might consider a (reputable) membership service that offers steep discounts at participating gyms and studios, perhaps better enabling you to find a class you like. Then again, if you're not into communal sweating, walk out the door and jog in your neighborhood. Or simply buy a jump rope; physical education instructors know that the best overall exercise for cardio strength is jumping rope. You may need to be a little creative to find an exercise regime that works for you. The main point is that you choose something you really like, because that way, you'll do it. And if you do choose a more social form of exercise (e.g., gym, tennis league, marathon team training, "boutique" boxing), you may even come across a potential exercise buddy out flexing his abs at exactly the same time as you.

Additionally, know that your efforts will reap benefits that far outweigh (sorry) your appearance: regular aerobic exercise has been conclusively shown to elevate mood and stave off depression. It also boosts mental acuity by efficient, increased blood flow to the brain. (I'd probably still be "stuck" trying to write much of the prose on these pages if not for the pronounced brain boosts I experienced after either lap swimming or jogging, in support of the reams of credible new research linking exercise to sharper thinking.) Feeling forgetful lately?

Exercise has recently been proven to improve memory as well. In a similar manner, exercise also helps prevent migraine headaches. A 2014 study of more than 1.4 million people showed that exercise even decreased the risk of thirteen forms of cancer, including breast, ovarian, and colon. Add that to the well-documented fact that exercise lowers risk of heart disease, the number-one killer of American women. *All told, exercise is truly an unparalleled, self-sustaining elixir not only for weight control, but also for overall well-being.* If there existed a pill that people could swallow and have the same results as exercise (living longer, feeling happier, looking better, etc.), it would truly be a miracle drug. It's suggested, therefore, that you make exercise a set part of your daily routine, and don't give yourself a choice about doing it. You wouldn't think twice about brushing your teeth, right? So let your oral hygiene set the standard for your "health hygiene" — i.e., exercise.

Insider Beauty Tips (You'll Thank Me)

In contrast to weight control, which typically involves lifestyle changes, here are the best of quick and easy fixes that I've gathered over the years by paying attention in a sun-kissed city where Hollywood studios, Malibu beaches, and certain Beverly Hills bodegas seem to breed beautiful women. First and foremost among these beauty basics is simply a great haircut. In an informal experiment, I showed ten men a headshot of the same woman with two different styles and shades of blonde hair, which was medium length in both photographs. One photo depicted the woman rocking platinum blonde straight hair (think: Naomi Watts); the other picture showed her with straw-colored, frizzed out hair (think: bad hair day by the beach). Not realizing it was the same person, all but two of the men deemed the "first woman" with the more flattering haircut and color prettier! (Of course none of the women test subjects were fooled.) A picture is worth a thousand words; find one of a style you like, and bring it to a salon with good Internet reviews. As for that California beach vibe, "sun-streaked" hair is youthful, beautiful, and natural looking at almost any age. For an inexpensive way to do it yourself, there are lots of leave-in hair lighteners on the market. (My favorite is "Sun Bum.") But if you're not quite as adventurous (or are unwilling to risk botched hair color), then try balayage, a process where highlights are painted on by hand in a salon. Many female Hollywood trendsetters use this technique to color their hair; it can make a plain face look foxy-pretty and a pleasant face look stunning.

While men are typically divided on whether a woman's face or body attracts them first, there's surprising male consensus regarding a woman's teeth. Specifically, one hundred men between the ages of twenty-one and fifty-five were anonymously polled as to what they notice first about a woman's facial features. Teeth were a close second to eyes as the most frequent facial feature named. Perhaps this is because attractive white teeth have the capacity to brighten up one's entire face. Just using a toothpaste containing baking soda (Arm & Hammer makes a good one), will improve the whiteness of your teeth over time. Or you might even consider applying bleaching gel at home, which can be just as effective and much less expensive than having it done in the dentist's office.

As for "popping" your eyes, regardless of their color or size, it's how you use mascara that makes all the difference. For example, applying mascara to the tip of your lashes first, and then going back and brushing the entire lash from the root on out makes your lashes appear especially long, likewise flattering your eyes. Yet another trick to open up your eyes is to substitute navy or royal blue mascara sometimes for black; print models swear by this. And layering any two colors of mascara lends a sultry, sexy look (think: Mila Kunis).

Equally important to highlighting your eyes as lashes are eyebrows. Have them professionally arched once and you'll notice how much prettier your eyes and face will look; then follow the line yourself. Makeup guru Sam Fine, who has made up the faces of many famed beauties, including Beyoncé, similarly advises, "If you want to bring attention from your smaller lip to your beautiful eyes, then that means a lash and beautiful brow." Generally speaking, Fine emphasizes drawing attention to your favorite feature. But even when "drawing attention," as I (again) advise just like with jewelry, less tends to be more, especially when it comes to eye shadows and blush. Remember, it's not about the makeup itself, it's about makeup making you look better.

And it's really not difficult to look better if you want, because in our digital age you can find some fairly good video demonstrations on nearly any cosmetic topic. (One that worked especially well for me was achieving the "pouty" lip: apply gloss only to the upper lip's Cupid 's bow and the dead center of the lower lip.) Are you a woman of color and feeling neglected by fair-complexioned makeup mavens? New beauty websites like blkgrn.com are loaded with additional specific tips for brown-skinned women too. Have fun experimenting, and you'll likely discover at least a few new makeup tricks that fit well into your lifestyle and look.

And I don't just mean for your face.

Nearly Naked

For a quick, flattering trick to showcase your body at its best, use a store-bought bronzer, or splurge on a customized spray tan applied by a technician in a tanning salon. This is a very easy, painless way to give your appearance an instant boost by imparting an attractive, healthy-looking glow to your skin. A body bronzer also works better than any magician's sorcery to banish cellulite, or at least camouflage it. For my dancer patients, who range from exotic dancers to classical ballerinas, their bronzer is their second skin. Notably, it's also the secret weapon of choice for *Dancing with the Stars* contestants to look shimmery-svelte in their skimpy costumes (the show reportedly goes through gallons of spray tan per season), and for *Sports Illustrated* swimsuit issue cover girls to give their skin a sexy, moist-looking sheen. And if you're olive-complexioned or darker, try applying bronzer lightly to your face as well. Friends and acquaintances will remark that you "look good" but won't know what's different.

Hollywood Beauty Basics (And How to Achieve)

- Face-flattering hair style (Great haircut)
- "Sun-kissed" hair color (Leave-in hair lightener or balayage)
- "Bright" smile (Teeth-whitening toothpaste and/or gel)
- Radiant skin (Bronzer or spray tan)
- Beautiful brows (Professionally arch once, then follow on own.)
- Long lashes (Apply mascara to lash tip *first*, then brush outward from root.)
- Eye "pop" for photos (Use navy or royal blue mascara.)
- Sultry eyes (Layer any two mascara colors.)
- Pouty lip (Gloss upper/lower lip centers *only.*)

Makeup as an Antidepressant

In addition to the obvious external advantages resulting from looking one's best, how women feel about their appearance almost always affects how they approach dating. As noted, the internal psychological lift accompanying an improved appearance can be especially empowering, but what's less obvious is makeup's role as a "double-hitter" in this regard. Specifically, if you're feeling down, go and play with some makeup: laboratory research reveals that merely experimenting with makeup such as lipsticks, eye shadows, and even nail polish significantly elevates mood in women experiencing mild depression. So in addition to helping us look better, makeup actually makes us feel better.

Note that according to the most recent industry statistics, American women spent approximately 42 billion dollars on cosmetics in 2016. However, many women are buying expensive brands that do exactly the same thing as the less expensive drugstore versions. What most women don't know is that many brands, pricey ones in particular, play on women's feelings of inadequacy by using unusually gorgeous women in their marketing campaigns. Sadly, a 2011 Dove research study, "The Real Truth about Beauty: Revisited" — to date the largest global study on women's relationship with beauty — found that only four percent of women worldwide think they're beautiful. To turn that thinking around, my personal favorite line comes from Carole King (who met more than her fair share of romantic heartache with resiliency and resolve): "You're beautiful as you feel."

Granted, it's tough to feel attractive when you're constantly inundated with the likes of women who appear to have won the looks lottery at birth. To note, in addition to cosmetic manufacturers' onslaught of "super-beauties" in their ads, popular culture also feeds women and girls impossible beauty standards. After all, how many of us who passed endless childhood hours with our Barbies awoke one day to a body that blossomed into the adult-size equivalent of a thirty-nine-inch bust and an eighteen-inch waist? Probably not many, unless Sofia Vergara is reading this, who by the way has been enlisted to hock nearly everything from furniture to, of course, cosmetics. This brings us full circle to not trying to look like someone else. But that doesn't mean that you shouldn't strive for a feel-good, looks-empowered best version of *you*.

Oh, and on an interestingly telling side note, as of February 2016, Barbie comes in three additional body types: "petite," "curvy," and "tall." So even Barbie is no longer trying to look like, well, Barbie.

Cosmetic Surgery: Consider Yourself Warned

No matter how hard they try, some women nevertheless are unable to reach a threshold level of satisfaction with their appearance. If this applies to you because of reasonable long-standing appearance issues — issues that can't be fixed with minimally invasive procedures — you may at least wish to consider cosmetic surgery. In this regard, "reasonable" means that trusted people in your life would recognize the same problem areas as you. If you're unsure, a good idea is to discuss your perceived problem area with a psychotherapist; he or she can better distinguish between objective cosmetic complaints and larger insecurities. For instance, a face-lift (rhytidectomy) won't make a sixty-five-year-old face look twenty-five, nor will it stop the aging process. Yet while your sexagenarian sister won't suddenly morph into a preternaturally young cosmetic clone, at the very least she can still improve on a perpetually "tired" look. Relatively new techniques involving laser or facial fillers such as Restylane also effectively address a range of aesthetic issues in a far less invasive manner than surgery.

If you eventually do decide on cosmetic surgery, be aware that unlike procedures such as Botox, facial plastic surgery is nonreversible; therefore, it's much better to spend time strategizing with the surgeon beforehand, rather than lamenting what "should have been done" afterward, when it's too late. Along these lines, noted Beverly Hills plastic surgeon Robert Hutcherson, MD, emphasizes that patients "need to feel that they aren't on a time clock." Similarly, a recent cosmetic surgeon/dinner party seatmate of mine, Robert Kotler, MD, (remember, I live in the "cosmetic surgery capital" of the country), extolled the value of good communication between doctor and patient as key to the best results. Hutcherson takes this even further, "Communicating well with the doctor means you have rapport, and rapport is a two-way street. The patient needs to feel that the surgeon is in touch with their goals, and the surgeon needs to understand what those goals are." To this end, I suggest writing down questions beforehand to refer to during your consultation, when emotion may throw you off track. And Hutcherson also recommends bringing in photographs, especially with new technology that allows analytic comparison with current, real-time photos of oneself regarding what can and can't be accomplished. Remember that plastic surgeons aren't magicians: they can dramatically improve your appearance, but don't expect them to change it completely.

Nor would you want them to. That said, if the size and/or shape of your nose has persistently bothered you for years, a "nose job" (rhinoplasty/nose reshaping) may well transform your entire face—and self-confidence, enabling you to enjoy your true "profile picture" for perhaps the first time. If you keep your expectations in check and carefully research your cosmetic surgical options, only then should you join the ranks of the millions of women in the United States who have had procedures. (According to the American Society of Plastic Surgeons, in 2017 alone: 300,378 women had breast augmentations; 246,354 had liposuction; and 218,924 had nose reshaping.) Given the noteworthy absence of corresponding patient satisfaction statistics in a medical field with largely subjective standards, however, your own due diligence will undoubtedly make a huge difference.

Dance: Ten; Looks: Three (Tits and Ass)

Ultimately, regardless of how men respond, your decision as to whether to change your appearance, even subtly, has to be based on how *you* wish to look and what you're comfortable with. Remember, men come and go, but your face and body remain with you forever. In other words, if you're going to take a scalpel to your precious, nature-given anatomy, do it for yourself and not just for the men in your life (or the men you hope to be in your life).

Let's take a moment to look at breasts. Say you're a small-breasted woman with Centerfold Envy. If so, the nearly epidemically common "boob job" will, in fact, most likely put a livelier bounce in your step—especially psychologically. Consider that author/producer Nora Ephron, arguably one of the preeminent literary feminists of the twentieth century, confided in a 1972 *Esquire* magazine essay that she would have been a "completely different person" had she "had [breasts]." She further elaborated, "[Some] men minded . . . [others] didn't. In any case, I always minded."

The problem with breasts is that no matter how many chest presses or extensions you do, they still won't plump up. Meaning that there probably isn't an effective "organic" alternative to having them done if they're really bothering you. In contrast, your gluteus maximus, or butt muscle, does respond very well to exercise. Therefore, if you're considering a less mainstream procedure such as buttock augmentation, also known as the Brazilian Butt Lift, you may want to opt instead for intense Stairmaster workouts together with a flattering pair of jeans — perhaps just as effective and far more safe.

Hot Stuff Playlist ♫
Beautiful/Christina Aguilera
Beautiful/Carole King
Dance: Ten; Looks: Three (Tits and Ass)/Marvin Hamlisch, Edward Kleban

Closing Thoughts:

Go Out and Kill It

*E*mpowerment is hot.

Today's empowered woman isn't obligingly just rolling over and taking it anymore. That applies to anything, whether it's a bad rap, bad dates, bad relationships, bad behavior — or bad sex. She stands up for herself.

Remember, feminism means you can make *any* of the same choices as men without recrimination. A new man whom you're excited about but, for whatever reason, doesn't wish to sleep with you yet isn't worrying about being rejected for that decision. In a far more common scenario, when you cave to a guy's potentially unwelcome pressure for sex just to hold onto him, you aren't exercising true choice (or feminism) at all; you're merely handing over the reins in the relationship. Plus, sleeping with a dating partner before you're really ready doesn't allow you to weed out jerky guys (who eventually bail anyway) from the good ones (read: committed) until you're emotionally invested and vulnerable. Put differently, if you initially refuse sex and a guy walks without even caring enough to wait and see what develops, it becomes immediately obvious that the dude's not your soul mate.

Then again, there simply may be times in a woman's life when her desire for physical intimacy isn't necessarily about finding a cosmic connection. So if you do choose to hook up right away with a particular man, do it because you really want to — not because you think you have to. At least try to avoid the guys who will disrespect you for many of the same choices they make all the time. Your instincts will help immensely in that regard, but only if you don't ignore them. Or obliterate them with Jell-O shots. And never, ever lose sight of your own self-respect and emotional well-being regardless of how blindsided you may be by some really smooth but toxic operators even your instincts couldn't have picked up on. Similarly, thinking longer term, no matter how great a guy looks on paper or how charming he comes across socially, none of that will eventually mean much if he's not trustworthy or kind.

As my dad used to say, there are no dress rehearsals for life. This is it. Insofar as romantic involvements, you'll do best if you embrace the entire oftentimes confounding process — including all the good and the not-so-good stuff that inevitably comes along. No matter where you may be on your journey, however, the following *Don't Sleep with Him Yet* critical takeaways will ultimately help you hit your own personal bull's-eye. My dear reader: *you got this.*

Dr. Lee's Love Lessons

- Date with your eyes wide open, but don't let fear of mistakes hold you back.
- Never settle for heartache.
- Be badass bold; think outside the box.
- Trust yourself; confidence trumps cowardice.
- Newfound resolve helps weaken emotional pain.
- Look to a romantic partner to enhance, not define your life.
- Believe in and assert your value.
- Don't people-please with sex or pretend you don't care.
- Communicate your needs while you practice empathy.
- Flirt openheartedly; enjoy your (and his) sensuality.

And always keep in mind that a good haircut never hurts.

Appendix 1

Empowering Steps Soundtrack: The Playlist

Can't Hold Us Down/Christina Aguilera	Introduction
Girls Just Wanna Have Fun/Cyndi Lauper	Introduction
Girl on Fire/Alicia Keys	Step 1
Respect Yourself/Melissa Etheridge	Step 1
I Am Woman (Hear Me Roar)/Helen Reddy	Step 1
You Gotta Be/Des'ree	Step 2
Flawless/Beyoncé	Step 2
Stronger/Brittany Spears	Step 2
Before He Cheats/Carrie Underwood	Step 3
Try/Pink	Step 3
When I'm Sixty-Four/Paul McCartney	Step 3
Audition (The Fools Who Dream)/Justin Hurwitz, Benj Pasek, Justin Paul	Step 3
Cabaret/Liza Minnelli	Step 4
Matchmaker, Matchmaker/Jerry Bock	Step 4
Blurred Lines/Robin Thicke, Pharrell Williams	Step 5

Old Friends/Simon and Garfunkel	Step 5
The Shadow of Your Smile/Tony Bennett	Step 5
Shadowboxer/Fiona Apple	Step 5
All About That Bass/Meghan Trainor	Step 6
Cupid/Sam Cooke	Step 6
The Look of Love/Burt Bacharach, Hal David	Step 6
Wicked Game/Chris Isaak	Step 7
Dancing in the Dark/Bruce Springsteen	Step 7
In Your Eyes/Peter Gabriel	Step 7
Shape of You/Ed Sheeran	Step 7
Someone Like You/Adele	Step 8
One More Night/Maroon 5	Step 8
Somebody That I Used to Know/Gotye	Step 8
Shake It Off/Taylor Swift	Step 8
With or Without You/U2	Step 9
Single Ladies/Beyoncé	Step 9
What's Love Got to Do with It/Tina Turner	Step 9
At Last/Etta James	Step 9
She Was Hot/Rolling Stones	Step 10
A Case of You/Joni Mitchell	Step 10
Your Body Is a Wonderland/John Mayer	Step 10
Beautiful/Christina Aguilera	Hot Stuff
Beautiful/Carole King	Hot Stuff

Dance: Ten; Looks: Three/Marvin Hamlisch, Edward Kleban	Hot Stuff
Like a Virgin/Madonna	Appendix 2
What a Girl Wants/Christina Aguilera	Appendix 2
Bad Romance/Lady Gaga	Appendix 2
SMS (Bangerz)/Miley Cyrus	Appendix 2
You Belong with Me/Taylor Swift	Appendix 2
Breathe/Taylor Swift	Appendix 2
Layla/Eric Clapton	Appendix 3
Something/George Harrison	Appendix 3
Rolling in the Deep/Adele	Appendix 3
And I Am Telling You I'm Not Going/ Jennifer Hudson	Appendix 3
Marilyn Monroe/Nicki Minaj	Appendix 3

Appendix 2

Top Picks: Iconic Generational Female Singers as Sexual Role Models

Baby Boomers: Madonna (Madonna Louise Ciccone, b. 1958)

Madonna taught blossoming boomers to celebrate their sexuality in a joyful, overtly provocative way. First came female expression through in-your-face hot clothing. Whether it was a lace-and-leather bustier, up-to-there miniskirt, or pair of sky-high stilettos, the message was less about the skin-baring outfits than the fact that strong, successful women could still flaunt their bodies. The Madonna signature style of wearing undergarments, like a bra, on the outside continues to survive — and thrive — today. And the BDSM-inspired look of many of her onstage outfits has also made it into the mainstream; once again, the take-home is in women's *power* over men versus sexual submission.

Later, as a forty-plus boomer herself, Madonna paved the way for "mature" women to have boy toys of their own (read: use young, hot guys for sex), while simultaneously winking at the sexual objectification of men that women themselves have forever endured. At sixty, she still beds much younger guys and can rock fishnet stockings and a thong with the best of them. Professor Camille Paglia from the University of the Arts noted, "Madonna has taught young women to be fully female and sexual while still exercising control over their lives." Perhaps not so much like a virgin though. In contrast to this blonde paragon of ambition's razor-sharp entrepreneurial savvy and creative control, Madonna's dating life appears far less focused. In addition to marriages to actor Sean Penn and producer Guy Ritchie, Madonna has been linked romantically to partners as far ranging as Hollywood heavyweights Warren Beatty, Antonio Banderas, and Willem Dafoe; political royalty John F. Kennedy Jr., "bad boy" singer Lenny Kravitz; comedian Sandra Berhnard; bisexual model, Tony Ward; rappers Vanilla Ice and Big Daddy Kane; basketball star/eccentric Dennis Rodman; and baseball legends Alex Rodriguez and Jose Canesco. To name just a *few*. Regardless of whether Madonna would do it all (or them all) again, many of Madonna's minions, now fifty and sixty-something-year-old highly accomplished women themselves, looked to her as a role model for their own varied sexual exploits.

Generation X: Christina Aguilera (b. 1980)

Christina Aguilera overcame early adversity in the form of a less than idyllic childhood to ultimately model her own version of sexy female uber-strength and confidence. Just like the nontraditional households of so many of her Gen X sisters, the singer was raised by a capable, determined single mother. But it's Aguilera's resolute, worked-hard-for-it ascent to mega success, despite the early psychological insults of a physically and emotionally abusive father, which truly sets a tremendously empowering example for all women. Aguilera's journey shows us that the path to "dreams come true" (or "what a girl wants") isn't necessarily an immediately clear one, nor is it without heartache. Nevertheless, this diva demonstrates the invaluable role of resilience, whether in overcoming the pain of a failed marriage or, on a lesser life note (so to speak), moving past the public embarrassment of missing a line from the national anthem during a Super Bowl game.

And Aguilera does it all with beauty, grace, and attitude; this former Mouseketeer oozes sensual female power in whichever persona she happens to choose, including a dark punk-diva, a burlesque kitten, and a Marilyn Monroe-esque bombshell. Touted as a sex symbol over the past decade by the *Los Angeles Times*, the *New York Times*, and *Maxim*, Aguilera also is a good example of "forty as the new thirty," not just because of her great looks, however enhanced, but also due to her passionate, zest-for-life exuberance and energy.

Generation X Runner-Up: Lady Gaga (Stefani Joanne Angelina Germanotta, b. 1986)

Although her birthdate is technically within the millennial range, Lady Gaga's personal background and pop cultural influence are more representative of Generation X. Specifically, the irreverence inherent in her most wildly memorable staged looks and lyrics belies Stefani Germanotta's traditional attitude toward love and romance. This is exactly in sync with her Gen X sisters, whose outward cynicism masks their conventionality. As Lady Gaga herself describes, "I am a real family girl. When it comes to love and loyalty, I am very old-fashioned." I surmise that the attention-grabbing (understatement) getups are just that: a highly successful strategic device by a smart entertainer. Lady Gaga realized early on that she would get much more mileage out of shock value than through attractive-in-her-own-way but not-so-classically-pretty looks. But that was then: this unparalleled powerhouse of a musical artist has recently let loose a remarkably classy, authentically beautiful woman — onstage and off. Stefani Germanotta is actually the total package of exotic-looking with brains to boot: there can never be a "Bad Romance" between Lady Gaga and her gazillions of adoring fans.

Millennials: Miley Cyrus (b. 1992)

A few years back Miley Cyrus seemed a sort of pop cultural scapegoat for whatever parents of female tweens and teens find objectionable, from provocative clothing to wanton sex. However, time ultimately turned this charismatically delightful, super talented singer's detractors into fans. Those paying close attention may have also noticed that Miley actually doesn't have a string of casual Hollywood hookups behind her, as do most of her soul sisters. In fact, this former Disney teen idol chooses to conduct her offstage love life far more traditionally than her sexualized stage presence would suggest. Consider Miley as a "closeted" monogamist who goes for long-term commitment and considers unfaithfulness a deal-breaker. To note, four years ago she broke off a first engagement to her fiancé due to reports of his "extracurricular" hookups. Sometimes, however, life does graciously offer second chances: the recently married couple appear to be happier than ever.

So despite her sexy manner of dress — and undress (recall Annie Liebowitz's 2008 nude-looking art photographs), this young beauty has shown women that they can push the envelope on racy, sexy outward image, yet still be a "good girl." Miley's performance art at the 2013 MTV Video Music Awards may have been about strutting her stuff onstage in latex underwear with a wagging tongue and oversized glove, but the art of her real life is long-term loyalty. Don't judge a book by its cover; nay, don't judge at all: Miley Cyrus proves the millennial motto that you can successfully forge your own path regarding relationships and personal style. Nor do you have to put up with mean-spirited critics — or cheating boyfriends. In the singer's own words, "If he's like that, I've got a world tour they need me at."

Millennial Runner-Up: Taylor Swift (b. 1990)

Taylor Swift is the torchbearer for anyone reading this book who at the moment may be sitting on the sidelines watching others have all the fun: it's never too late to start working hard and believing in *you*. The first woman ever to win the highly coveted Grammy Album of the Year award twice, Taylor has proven that smart girls end up much hotter than complacent, short-sighted "cheer captains," and that persistence pays off.

In spades.

Notably, the then-fourteen-year-old aspiring performer from Reading, Pennsylvania, purportedly endured rejection after rejection at the doors of Nashville studios before one record label finally took a chance on the eighth grader. And boy, talk about the value of optimistically taking reasoned chances (Step 2). According to *Billboard* stats, Taylor Swift has sold over 26 million albums and 75 million digital downloads, with a net worth estimated by *Forbes* of over 220 million dollars. But judging from the lyrical laments in her songs (think: "I can't breathe without you, but I have to breathe without you, but I have to breathe without you"), the skinny blonde would be wise to pay particular attention to Step 8: Letting Go: When and How to Move On—or Move In.

Appendix 2 Playlist ♫
Like a Virgin/Madonna
What a Girl Wants/Christina Aguilera
Bad Romance/Lady Gaga
SMS (Bangerz)/Miley Cyrus
You Belong with Me/Taylor Swift
Breathe/Taylor Swift

Appendix 3

Dating–Sexual Style Inventory (DSSI)
Are You a "Layla," "Adele," "Effie," or "Marilyn"?

Please answer "Yes" or "No" to the following 15 questions. (Scoring and description of your dating-sexual style can be found on pages 218 through 220.)

1. Did you lose your virginity before the age of eighteen?
2. Have you ever found yourself still wondering where you stand with a guy after at least a few months of dating?
3. Do you ever feel you owe a man sex or that it would somehow be "impolite" to refuse him?
4. Has it been over two years since you've been romantically involved with someone, whether or not you've slept together?
5. Do you often find yourself sleeping with a new man before you're truly ready?
6. Are you involved with a partner who says he cares for you but never says he loves you?
7. Do you feel that you must have sex with a new dating partner in order to hold his interest?
8. Does your confidence fall apart when it comes to men compared to other realms of life?

9. Do you panic when you haven't heard from a dating partner for a few days after seeing him?
10. Have you ever felt pressured to have unwanted sex or found yourself unable to back out for fear of angering your partner?
11. Have you ever caved to a partner's request for a sexual act you're uncomfortable with and then regretted it afterward?
12. Do you find yourself unhappy when there's not a special man in your life?
13. Is it rare that you achieve orgasm despite regular or frequent sex?
14. Are your own needs and wants (not just sexual) presently dismissed or ignored by a dating partner?
15. Has sex become mostly meaningless or empty for you, even though it may not have started out that way?

DSSI Scoring

To discover your dating-sexual style, total the number of "Yes" responses.

The Layla: 0–3 "Yes" responses. Your dating-sexual style is, put simply, that of a goddess. Like the Eric Clapton song of the same name (inspired by his friend's wife and then-model, Pattie Boyd) you already have men down on their knees "begging, darling, please." You appreciate sensuality in yourself and others, but men are also drawn to you apart from sex. To wit, "Something in the way she moves, attracts me like no other lover." George Harrison wrote these lyrics, and one of the Beatles' best love songs ever, for his wife at the time; who else but rock muse Pattie Boyd (whom Mick Jagger admitted he tried unsuccessfully to seduce for years—and who eventually married Eric Clapton). Since you tend to attract all sorts of men (including those who are unavailable), don't ignore red flags, and also listen closely to your instincts.

Pay particular attention to: Flirting with Disaster (Step 7), and 10 Ways to Keep the Sex Going Strong (Step 10).

The Adele: 4–6 "Yes" responses. Even though you sometimes get stuck in Heartbreak mode, you manage to pick yourself up and get back in the game. You navigate life with an upbeat attitude that prevents a few depressing detours from derailing personal goals such as love and commitment from the right guy. What's more, you pay attention and learn from past experience. It may take a while, but to borrow from this dating style's namesake, the "fever pitch in your heart" finally allows you to "see things crystal clear." Keep forging on, and someday you *will* have it all.

Pay particular attention to: Optimism (Step 2), Men Who Are Trouble (Step 3), and 10 Best Heartbreak-Busters (Step 8).

The Effie: 7–9 "Yes" responses. You are a giving person— but perhaps a bit too giving when it comes to sleeping with men. Fear of rejection or abandonment is often a motivating force for you in relationships. This dating style is rife with silent resentment and debilitating frustration as you consistently put your partners' needs before your own. Learn to rev up self-confidence and assert *your* wishes early on to the men whom you date, instead of automatically acquiescing to theirs. That way you won't find yourself having to implore a man à la *Dreamgirls'* Effie: "And you, and you, you're gonna love me," because it's *him*, not you, who should be doing the groveling.

Pay particular attention to: Respect Yourself (Step 1), Lucky 7 Confidence Boosters (Step 2), Hookups That Unhinge (Step 5), and Don't People-Please with Sex (Step 9).

The Marilyn: 10–15 "Yes" responses. Although you may be a beautiful, talented woman, your talents do not extend to dating. In fact, your dating-sexual style has deteriorated to its present level of disastrous. You use sex like a lasso to tighten your hold on men, but they either get strangled or slip through the rope. You become increasingly disillusioned at each new romantic disappointment, as you wonder why others, but not you, seem to get what they want. What's more, you're throwing away your true potential for rewarding relationships. As experience has taught Nicki Minaj: "It's like all the good things/They fall apart like, like Marilyn Monroe." Which means it's finally time to turn your train wreck of a dating life around before the next major crash.

Pay particular attention to: *all* the Steps.

Appendix 3 Playlist ♫
Layla/Eric Clapton
Something/George Harrison
Rolling in the Deep/Adele
And I Am Telling You I'm Not Going/Jennifer Hudson
Marilyn Monroe/Nicki Minaj

Appendix 4

"SEX" Exercise for Focused Sensuality

The following exercise works so well precisely because it is highly erotic with minimal involvement of sexual private parts (other than visually). It's actually the *sensual* focus that's so pleasurable. In fact, the exercise was inspired by Masters and Johnson's sensate focus technique to increase physical intimacy without performance pressures (i.e., men's erections; women's orgasms.) The script is intended to be unisex, so that partners take turns as recipients whose only "job" is to tune into their own experience as they take in the touch.

Here you go:

First, find a quiet room — the bedroom works well here — and dim the lights to where it's dark yet you can still see. Slowly undress in front of one another, but you may not touch, at least not yet. Have your partner, termed "the recipient," lie on their stomach. Then begin to gently massage your partner's back, applying just enough pressure to feel the sensation of your hands pressing into flesh. Move your hands very slowly. Let them wander to the back of your partner's neck. Caress the ears, and work your way, once again, down the back to the buttocks, legs, and feet. Alternate using your now-magical hands and lips in any way you choose — you may involve your tongue as well. (Remember, however, the recipient is lying on their stomach; this is a sensual exercise, *not* oral sex.)

Don't allow your mind to wander or to think about anything other than the present moment and what you're doing. Focus rather on the sensations you feel throughout your own body when you are touching and stroking your partner's bare skin. When your fingers have reached the toes, work your hands back on up over the soles of the feet, applying gentle but firm pressure. Let your hands and mouth travel to the recipient's calves; alternate manual kneading/massaging with light kisses. Hang out here for a while and let yourself get turned on by the firmness and strength of your partner's calves. Once your hands make their way farther up, gently stroke the inside of your partner's thighs with your fingertips before you gradually press harder into the fleshiest part of the legs. You are very close, but be sure you don't touch any genitals. Take as long as you'd like to massage your partner's inner thighs. Afterward, move your hands back to the outside of the recipient's legs, which you pet using the palm and heel of your hands. Then gently trace, with a light back-and-forth motion of your fingers, the place where the buttocks meets the legs. Pause there momentarily before letting your hands and mouth continue their journey back up the small of the recipient's lower back. Let your parted lips linger anywhere along the way for a brief moment before heading all the way up the back to the shoulders. Massage the shoulders for a bit before moving on to the lower neck, then up the neck to the scalp. Spend some time caressing and massaging your partner's scalp and the crown of their head. Finish by running your fingers through your partner's hair.

Side note: For the most effective results, use the exercise as a springboard for your own experimentation and improvisation. Also, for a full-on sensual experience, add oils and/or scents as discussed in Step 10.

Appendix 5

Coming to Terms (Glossary)

Badass: A smart, confident woman who owns her choices and isn't afraid to take risks. She is kind and empathic, but never a doormat. The badass woman embraces life with a sense of vitality and hopefulness regardless of the hand she's dealt. (Step 1, page 19; Step 2, page 28)

Clueless: A woman who bases her interpersonal behaviors and choices on blind conformity to what others are doing (or on the general perception of what they're doing). Peer pressure and people-pleasing often negatively influence important decisions such that authentic desires and dreams go unfulfilled. (Introduction, pages 1, 4)

COME: An attitudinal acronym to remind you that that Confidence, Optimism, Mindfulness, and Enthusiasm are not only key to successful dating, but will also enable you to reach (or COME to) a new, markedly enhanced enjoyment of life as a whole. (Step 2, page 28)

Companion Coconspirators: Dating partners who enjoy each other's company and companionship but don't want a more serious, long-term commitment. Although this is increasingly prevalent, a majority of today's women still seek soul mates. (Step 1, page 18)

Compare-and-Despair Syndrome: A new psychological malady brought about by social media whereby women compare their less-than-perfect lives to other women's mostly idealized versions of reality. The cure: take a break from Facebook and Instagram. (Step 2, page 31)

Date Rape: When men you know lacking both conscience and impulse control selectively "forget" the meaning of no. What some men have trouble grasping is that just because hookup culture is acceptable, that doesn't mean it's okay for them to push for an (unwanted) hookup with you. (Step 5, pages 85-86)

DUMB Communication: Communication that is **D**istorted, **U**nspoken, **M**isleading, and/or **B**otched. Frequently results in a woman not getting her needs met in a relationship or being unexpectedly dumped. (Step 8, page 133)

FLIRT: A specific skill-oriented method of flirting based on the neuroscience of attraction and romantic love. Guaranteed to infuse a sure shot of feel-good fun between two people or raise the stakes on an already existing attraction. (Step 7, page 111)

Friend Zone: What you do to a guy who you can't ever imagine having sex with. But don't think for a moment he stops imagining what sex would be like with you. (Step 5, page 75)

Hook Up: Don't do this with a random guy you meet unless you know it won't bother you if you hardly hear from him afterward. Which also means you have to stop checking your phone so much the next day. (See also "Unhinge.") (Step 5, pages 78-83; Step 9, page 152)

Hookup Fatigue: For women, casual sexual hookups cease to be much fun when the adventure and excitement wear off, and a more meaningful connection is desired. For men, sex often tends to become increasingly less gratifying with multiple casual partners. (Step 9, pages 146-147, 149)

I Care about You (in the absence of "I'm in love with you"): I am not in this for the long haul. (Step 8, page 134).

"In Like": It's the same as "I care about you," but without the backstory. Forget having a long-term romantic relationship with a guy you're sleeping with who (still) feels that way about you. (Step 5, page 76)

Lick-Taste-Kiss-Suck: All sensually focused acts. Whisper these words in your partner's ear at an *in*appropriate time: arousal guaranteed. (Step 10, page 185)

Lifeground: The totality of a person's core values, goals, ambitions, attitudes, lifestyle, experiences, and cultural choices. Compatible lifegrounds help foster a strong connection between dating partners subsequent to initial physical attraction. (Step 4, page 68)

Misguided: A woman who erroneously believes that women and men are psychosexually wired exactly alike. This is often to her detriment in the romantic arena. (Step 9, pages 150-151)

Narcissist: He captivates (baits?) you with charm, but soon callously disregards even the most basic of your needs. If you're not sure whether you're involved with a (pathological) narcissist, pay close attention to what your partner does versus what he says — because what the narcissist does is all about himself. (Step 3, pages 53-54)

Neathage: The underside of a woman's breasts, particularly when exposed by a crop top with no bra. Stick to subtle cleavage in your profile picture, proven to gain 49 percent more responses than the average photo. (Note: creepy guys with no filter are going to be inappropriate no matter what.) (Step 6, page 96)

Non-Swimsuit-Issue: Most women's body types. Once they have you naked, men don't care. (Step 10, pages 179-180)

(The) Not-So-Secret "Secret": A person's positive attitude along with enthusiasm for life makes her responsible for her own happiness and draws others to her as well. Touted by some life coaches as "revelatory," but actually a classic hallmark of positive psychology. (Step 2 page 37)

Out-of-Box: Select places and activities outside of your daily routine (including work) where you could meet potential dating partners. Out-of-box strategizing, as well as experimenting with dating apps, brings your, um, other "box" new possibilities. (Step 4, page 62)

Phenethylamine (PEA): The brain's own amphetamine-like "drug" of choice, which is released during a powerful attraction to a dating partner. Causes severe addiction in which the person becomes "hooked" on the object of their attraction, resulting in love-crazy behaviors. (Step 7, page 110; Step 9, page 160; Step 10, pages 180, 183)

Players: One of several categories of men who will almost certainly end up hurting you. Players are motivated primarily by their own sexual gratification and will say nearly anything to sleep with you before they move on. (Step 3, pages 52-53; Step 8, pages 130-131)

SEX: **S**avor, **E**xplore, and **"X"**cite one another sensually for the *best* sex ever. (Step 10, page 177; Appendix 4, page 221)

Softboy: Similar to a player, this mostly millennial man lures you in by appealing to your emotions. He acts like he's ready for a relationship (and sometimes even thinks he is), until he inevitably changes his mind. (Introduction, page 4; Step 3, page 53)

Targeted Rejection: A loss that is especially devastating because it is deliberately directed at one person *alone*. For instance, being the only one fired at work, or being dropped by a guy you really like. (Consider: "dejection" equals *de*pression plus re*jection*.) (Step 8, page 136)

Testosterone: The hormone that men have twenty times more of than women and, depending on their age, is responsible for them thinking about and/or pursuing sex near constantly. Women who seek commitment should not rush to scratch a man's testosterone "itch." (Step 9, page 152)

Touch-and-Tease: The "T" in FLIRT. Nice. (Step 7, page 118)

Unhinge: To distance oneself from someone after hooking up. When it's men who do the distancing, it leads their partners to become (emotionally) unhinged — as in unhappy, angry, and/or confused. (Step 5, pages 78-83)

Virtual Stranger: Your new cyber buddy whom you are in love with — despite the fact that you've never met. Proceed with caution. (Step 6, pages 104-105)

BIBLIOGRAPHY

Josh M. Ackerman, Vladas Griskevicius, and Norman P. Li, "Let's Get Serious: Communicating Commitment in Romantic Relationships," *Journal of Personality and Social Psychology* 100, no. 6 (2011): 1079-1094.

Sandy Banks, "After 36 Years It's Time to Say Thanks and Goodbye to Readers," *Los Angeles Times*, December 26, 2015.

Greg Behrendt and Liz Tuccillo, *He's Just Not That into You: The No-Excuses Truth to Understanding Guys*. New York: Simon and Schuster, 2004.

Sara L. Bengtsson, Raymond J. Dolan, and Richard E. Passingham, "Priming for Self-Esteem Influences the Monitoring of One's Own Performance," *Social Cognitive and Affective Neuroscience* 6, no. 4 (2011): 417–25.

Jessica Bennett and Daniel Jones, "45 Stories of Sex and Consent on Campus," *New York Times*, May 10, 2018.

Joe Biden, "It's On Us" campaign conference call, October 28, 2015.

Cory Birkett, "Won't Leave the House without Makeup? Blame the Marketing," FYILiving.com, September 23, 2011, http:// fyiliving.com/health-news/wont-leave-the-house-without-makeup-blame-manipulative-marketing/.

Deborah Blum, *Sex on the Brain: The Biological Differences between Men and Women*. New York: Viking, 1997.

Val Brown, "High End Matchmakers Dish on Dating," *Huffington Post*, November 17, 2011.

Elizabeth E. Bruch and M. E. J. Newman, "Aspirational Pursuit of Mates in Online Dating Markets," *Science Advances* 4, no.8 (August 8, 2018).

D. M. Busby, J. S. Carrol, and B. J. Willoughby, "Compatibility or Restraint? The Effects of Sexual Timing on Marriage and Relationships," *Journal of Family Psychology* (December 2010): 766–74.

David M. Buss, *The Evolution of Desire: Strategies of Human Mating*. New York: Basic Books, 1994.

Rhonda Byrne, *The Secret*. New York: Atria Books, 2006.

Gregory Luis Carter, Anne C. Campbell, and Steven Muncer, "The Dark Triad Personality: Attractiveness to Women," *Personality and Individual Differences*, 2013.

Centers for Disease Control and Prevention, "Chlamydia Fact Sheet," Cohabitation, Marriage, Divorce, and Remarriage Series, Report 23, no. 22 (2002).

Centers for Disease Control and Prevention, "National Marriage and Divorce Rate Trends 2000–2011," NCHS National Vital Statistics Systems, 2012.

Michael Ceo and Niki Ceo, *Couples and Affairs: Managing the Clinical Challenges*. Brentwood, TN: Cross Country Education, 2009.

Kenneth Champeon, "The Floating World," ThingsAsian. com, November 3, 2002, http://www.thingsasian.com/ stories-photos/2130.

Seth Cline, "Oops! Most Homemade Pornography Ends Up Online," *US News and World Report*, 2012.

David S. Cloud, "Pentagon Reports Sharp Rise in Military Sexual Assaults," *Los Angeles Times*, May 7, 2013.

Mark Cook and Robert McHenry, *Sexual Attraction*. New York: Pergamon Press, 1978.

Claude Crépault, *L'imaginaire Erotique et Ses Secrets*. Québec City: Presses de l'Université du Quebec, 1981.

Kirby Dick, Amy Ziering, Amy Herdy, Regina Kulick Scully, Paul Blavin, et al., 2015. *The Hunting Ground*.

X. Dai, P. Dong, and J. Jia, "When Does Playing Hard to Get Increase Romantic Attraction?" *Journal of Experimental Psychology: General,"* 143 (2014): 521-526.

Gavin de Becker, *The Gift of Fear*. New York: Dell, 1997.Andrea L. Dunn, Madhukar Trivedi, James B. Kampert, Camillia G. Clark, and Heather O. Chambliss, "Exercise Treatment for Depression," *Journal of Preventative Medicine* 28, no. 1 (January 2005): 1–8.

Naomi Eisenberger, "The Pain of Social Disconnection: Examining the Shared Neural Underpinnings of Physical and Social Pain," *Nature Reviews Neuroscience* 13 (2012): 421–34.

Paula England and Jonathan Marc Bearak, "The Sexual Double Standard and Gender Differences in Attitudes Toward Casual Sex among U.S. University Students," *Demographic Research 30, 46: 1327-1338*.

Nora Ephron, "A Few Words about Breasts," *Esquire*, May 1972.

Nora Ephron, *I Remember Nothing and Other Reflections*. New York: Alfred A. Knopf, 2010.

Eli J. Finkel, Paul W. Eastwick, Benjamin R. Karney, Harry T. Reis, and Susan Sprecher, "Online Dating: A Critical Analysis from the Perspective of Psychological Science," *Journal of Psychological Science in the Public Interest* 13, no. 1 (2012): 3-66.

Michael B. First, ed. *Diagnostic and Statistical Manual of Mental Disorders, Fifth Ed*. Washington, DC: American Psychiatric Association, 2013.

Donna Freitas, *The End of Sex: How Hookup Culture Is Leaving a Generation Unhappy, Sexually Unfulfilled, and Confused about Intimacy*. New York: Basic Books, 2013.

Patricia A. Ganz and Gail A. Greendale, "Female Sexual Desire — Beyond Testosterone," *Journal of the National Cancer Institute* 99, no. 9 (2007): 659–61.

Abigail Geiger and Gretchen Livingston, "8 Facts about Love and Marriage in the US," *Fact Tank News in the Numbers* (Pew Research Center, February 13, 2018).

Malcolm Gladwell, *Blink*. New York: Little, Brown and Co., 2005.

Gian Gonzaga, "How You Meet Your Spouse Matters," *The Science of Love* (eHarmony blog), February 20, 2011, http://www.eharmony.com/blog/2011/02/10/how-you-meet-your-spouse-matters/#.VINWRGTF_nI.

Adrian Gostick and Chester Elton, *The Carrot Principle*: *How the Best Managers Use Recognition to Engage Their People, Retain Talent, and Accelerate Performance*. New York: Simon and Schuster, 2009.

Daniel S. Hamermesh, *Beauty Pays: Why Atttractive People Are More Successful*. Princeton: Princeton University Press, 2011.

Kenneth G. Henshall, *A History of Japan:From Stone Age to Superpower*. London: MacMillan, 1999.

Jenny A. Higgens and Jennifer Hirsch, "The Pleasure Deficit: Revisiting the 'Sexuality Connection' in Reproductive Health," *International Family Planning Perspectives* 33, no. 3 (2007): 24–27.

Penelope M. Huang, Pamela J. Smock, Wendy D. Manning, and Cara A. Bergstrom-Lynch, "He Said, She Said: Gender and Cohabitation," *Journal of Family Issues* 32, no. 7 (2011): 876-905.

A. H. Iliffe, "A Study of Preferences in Feminine Beauty," *British Journal of Psychology* 51, no. 3 (April 13, 2011): 267–73.

Emma Jacobs, "A Lively Romp through the Internet Dating Marketplace" (Review of *Love in the Time of Algorithms: What Technology Does to Meeting and Mating* by Dan Slater), *Los Angeles Times*, February 3, 2013.

Jen Kalaidis, "The GOP Feminista," The Next Great Generation (TNGG) website, October 18, 2010, http://www.thenextgreat-generation.com/2010/10/18/the-gop-feministsta/.

Nancy Kalish, *Lost and Found Lovers: Facts and Fantasies of Rekindled Romances*. New York: William Morrow & Company, 1997.

Helen Singer Kaplan, *The New Sex Therapy: Active Treatment of Sexual Dysfunctions*. New York: Brunner/Mazel, 1974.

Soumya Karlamangla, "STD Cases Reaching All-Time Highs in US, California," *Los Angeles Times*, November 19, 2015.

Jill L. Kays and Alicia Tomasulo, "Working with Cohabitating Couples: Commitment Is Key," Regent University Hope Research Project, http://www.hopecouples.com/resources/Strategy_Guides/Working%20with%20Cohabitating%20Couples.pdf.

Gerrick D. Kennedy, "A Healing Mission: Mary J. Blige is back to form on her latest album, 'Strength of a Woman,' baring her soul about heartbreak, faith and survival," *Los Angeles Times*, May 9, 2017.

Robert Kotler, *Secrets of a Beverly Hills Cosmetic Surgeon: The Expert's Guide to Safe, Successful Surgery*. Beverly Hills: Ernest Mitchell, 2003.

Ethan Kross, Marc G. Merman, Walter Mischel, Edward El. Smith, and Tor D. Wager, "Social Rejection Shares Somatosensory Receptors with Physical Pain," *Proceedings of the National Academy of Sciences of the United States of America* 108, no. 15 (2011): 6,270–75.

Laura Kubzansky and Rebecca Thurston, "Emotional Vitality and Incident Corollary Heart Disease," *Archives of General Psychiatry* 64, no. 12 (2007): 1393-1401.

Robert Kurzban and Jason Weeden, "HurryDate: Mate Preferences in Action," *Evolution and Human Behavior* 26 (2005): 227–44.

Erin Kutz, "Coffee Meets Bagel Takes Flash Sales Approach to Online Dating in New York and Boston," *Xconomy*, August 1, 2012.

Julen H. Lallement, Katrina Kuss, Peter Trautner, Bernd Weber, Armin Falk, and Klaus Fliessbach, "Effort Increases Sensitivity to Reward and Loss Magnitude in the Human Brain," *Social Cognitive and Affective Neuroscience* (2012).

Edward O. Laumann, John H. Gagnon, Robert T. Michael, and Stuart Michaels, "The National Health and Social Life Survey, United States," Health and Medical Care Archives 06647 (1992).

I-Min Lee and Luc Djousse, "Physical Activity and Weight Gain Prevention," *Journal of the American Medical Association* 12 (2010): 1,173–79.

D. Marazziti, H. S. Akiskal, A. Rossi, and G. B. Cassano, "Alteration of the Platelet Serotonin Transporter in Romantic Love," *Psychological Medicine* 29 (1999): 741–45.

Dale Markowitz, "Hinge's CEO Says a Good App Relies on Vulnerability, Not Algorithms," *Washington Post*, September 29, 2017.

Robert Martin, *How We Do It: The Evolution and Future of Human Reproduction.* New York: Basic Books, 2013.

William H. Masters and Virginia E. Johnson, *Human Sexual Response.* New York: Bantam Books, 1966.

Justin McCurry, "Career Geisha Outgrow the Stereotype," *The Age*, December 11, 2005.

Marta Meana, "Elucidating Women's (Hetero) Sexual Desire: Definitional Challenges and Content Expansion," *Journal of Sex Research* 47 (2010): 104–22.

Cyndy Meston and David Buss, *Why Women Have Sex: The Psychology of Sex in Women's Own Voices*. New York: Times Books, 2009.

Lisa J. Mogilanski, "Why I'm Uncomfortable with the Hookup Culture," *USA Today*, May 26, 2013.

Anna Moore, "How Tinder Took me From Serial Monogamy to Casual Sex," *The Guardian*, September 28, 2014.

Monica Moore and Diana Butler, "Predictive Aspects of Nonverbal Courtship Behavior in Women," *Semiotica*, 3 (1989): 205-215.

Richard L. Moreland and Robert B. Zajonc, "Exposure Effects in Person Perception: Familiarity, Similarity, and Attraction," *Journal of Experimental Social Psychology* 18 (1982): 395–415.

Paul H. Morris, Jenny White, Edward R. Morrison, and Kayleigh Fisher, "High Heels as Supernormal Stimuli: How Wearing High Heels Affects Judgements of Female Attractiveness," *Journal of Evolution and Human Behavior* 34 no. 3 (May, 2013): 176-181.

Michael L. M. Murphy, George M. Slavich, Nicolas Rohleder, and Gregory E. Miller, "Targeted Rejection Triggers Differential Pro- and Anti-inflammatory Gene Expression in Adolescents as a Function of Social Status," *Clinical Psychological Science* (2012).

Nena O'Neill and George O'Neill, *Open Marriage: A New Lifestyle for Couples*. New York: M. Evans, 1972.

NIH Report, "Drug Facts: Club Drugs (GHB, Ketamine, and Rohypnol)," National Institute on Drug Abuse, July 2010.

Office on Women's Health, US Department of Health and Human Services, "Date Rape Fact Sheet," July 2012.

Alice Park, "Does Online Dating Make It Harder to Find 'the One'?" *Time* website, February 7, 2012, http://healthland.time.com/2012/02/07/does-online-dating-make-it-harder-to-find-the-one/.

Pamela Paul, "Relationship Status: In a 'Stayover,'" *New York Times*, August 19, 2011, http://www.nytimes.com/2011/08/21/fashion/the-stayover-as-a-relationship.html?_r=0.

Barbara Pease and Allan Pease, *The Definitive Book of Body Language*. New York: Bantam Dell, 2006.

Lisa A. Phillips, "Getting Close," *Psychology Today* 50, no. 1, (February, 2017).

Ann Powers, "Props Mistress: Christina Aguilera Dons Every Diva Role as She Pays Her Respect and Earns It Too," *Los Angeles Times*, March 7, 2007, http://articles.latimes.com/2007/mar/07/entertainment/et-aguilera7.

René T. Proyer and Willibald Ruch, "The Virtuousness of Adult Playfulness: The Relation of Playfulness with Strengths of Character," *Psychology of Well-Being: Theory, Research, and Practice* (2011): 1–4.

Mark Regnerus and Jeremy Uecker, *Premarital Sex in America: How Young Americans Meet, Mate, and Think about Marrying*. New York: Oxford University Press, 2007.

Laura Reston, "Is Hinge the New Tinder?" *Boston Globe*, August 15, 2014, http://www.boston.com/business/2014/08/15/hinge-the-new-tinder/story.html.

Galena K. Rhoades, Scott M. Stanley, and Howard J. Markman, "Pre-engagement Cohabitation and Gender Asymmetry in

Marital Commitment," *Journal of Family Psychology* 20 (2006): 553–60.

Galena K. Rhoades, Scott M. Stanley, and Howard J. Markman, "Sliding vs. Deciding: Inertia and the Premarital Cohabitation Effect," *Family Relations* 55 September 7, 2006.

Max Ritvo, "The Prank Your Body Plays on Life," WNYC Podcast, *Only Human*, July 12, 2016.

Christian Rudder, "The Four Big Myths of Profile Pictures," *OkTrends: Dating Research from OkCupid*, January 10, 2010, http://blog.okcupid.com/index.php/the-4-big-myths-of-profile-pictures/.

Kelefa Sanneh, "The New Season/Music; Idol Returns, Her Image Remade," *New York Times*, February 13, 2012, http://www.nytimes.com/2002/09/08/arts/the-new-season-music-idol-returns-her-image-remade.html?pagewanted=all.

Martin Seligman and James Pawelski, "Positive Psychology," *Psychological Inquiry* (2003): 159–163.

Wendy Shalit, *A Return to Modesty: Discovering the Lost Virtue*. New York: Touchstone, 2000.

Eugene Shippen and William Fryer, *The Testosterone Syndrome: The Critical Factor for Energy, Health, and Sexuality – Reversing the Male Menopause*. New York: M. Evans and Co., 1998.

Aaron Smith and Maeve Duggan, "Online Dating and Relationships," *Pew Research Center's Internet and American Life Project* (Pew Research Center, 2013).

Anthony Smith, A. Lyons, J. Ferris, J. Richters, M. Pitts, J. Shelley, and J. M. Simpson, "Sexual and Relationship Satisfaction among Heterosexual Men and Women: The Importance of Desired Frequency of Sex," *Journal of Sex and Marital Therapy* 37, no. 2 (2011): 104–115.

Graham Smith, "Women Really DO Find the Silent, Brooding Type Sexier: Scientists Discover Happy Men Are 'Significantly Less Attractive,'" *Daily Mail* website, May 24, 2011, http://www.dailymail.co.uk/sciencetech/article-1390319.

Springer, "Men Choose Romance Over Success," *ScienceDaily*, http://www.sciencedaily.com/releases/2007/08/070828110650.htm.

Lana Staheli, *Affair-Proof Your Marriage: Understanding, Preventing and Surviving an Affair.* New York: Cliff Street Books, 1998.

Kenneth Starr, "Special Report: The Starr Report Narrative," Washingtonpost.com, 1998, http://www.washington-post.com/wp-srv/politics/special/clinton/icreport/6nar-ritii.htm.

Statista, "Revenue of the Cosmetic/Beauty Industry in the United States from 2002 to 2016," December 3, 2018, http://www.statist.com/topics/ 1008/cosmeticsindustry.

Mai-Ly N. Steers, Robert E. Wickham, and Linda K. Acitelli, "Seeing Everyone Else's Highlight Reels: How Facebook Usage Is Linked to Depressive Symptoms," *Journal of Social and Clinical Psychology* 33 no. 8 (2014): 701–31.

Kat Stoeffel, "It Doesn't Have to Be Rape to Suck," *New York Magazine* website, October 6, 2014, http://nymag.com/thecut/2014/10/doesnt-have-to-be-rape-to-suck.htm.

Kate Taylor, "Sex on Campus: She Can Play that Game, Too," *New York Times*, July 12, 2013.

Shelley E. Taylor and Jonathan D. Brown, "Illusion and Well-Being: A Social Psychological Perspective on Mental Health," *Psychological Bulletin* 103, no. 2 (1988): 193–210.

Jean Twenge, Ryne Sherman, and Brooke Wells, "Declines in Sexual Frequency Among American Adults, 1989 to 2014" *Archives of Sexual Behavior* 46, no. 8 (2017): 2389-2401.

Various contributors, "2003 'Hot 100,'" *Maxim*, May 1, 2003.

VHI, "100 Sexiest Artists," 2002.

Wendy Walsh, *The 30-Day Love Detox: Cleansing Yourself of Bad Boys, Cheaters, and Men Who Won't Commit.* New York: Rodale, 2013.

Morley Winograd and Michael D. Hais, *Millennial Momentum: How a New Generation Is Remaking America.* New Brunswick, New Jersey: Rutgers University Press, 2011.

Naomi Wolf, "The Porn Myth," *New York Magazine*, October 20, 2003.

Bekah Wright, "Bruins in Love," *UCLA Magazine*, January 1, 2012, http://magazine.ucla.edu/features/bruins-in-love/.

David Xu, Ronald Cenfetelli, and Karl Aquino, "The Influence of Media Cue Multiplicity on Deceivers and Those Who Are Deceived," *Journal of Business Ethics* 106, no. 3 (2012): 337–52.

Robert B. Zajonc, "Attitudinal Effects of Mere Exposure," *Journal of Personality and Social Psychology* 9 (1968): 1–27.

ABOUT THE AUTHOR

*N*ancy F. Lee, PhD, is a clinical psychologist in private practice in Beverly Hills, California. A 2015 Vitals Patients' Choice Award recipient, her warm approach and incisive, practical insights have made her a favorite among patients. In addition to Dr. Lee's unique blend of clinical and academic dating and relationship expertise, her practice covers a wide range of behavioral health issues from depression and anxiety to male/female psychosexual desire and functioning. Notably, Dr. Lee is considered a leading practitioner of cognitive-behavioral therapy.

Dr. Lee is known as a lively, dynamic speaker, whether presenting before a group of medical personnel or to cyber-audiences hungry for advice on love. She especially enjoys leading student discussion forums covering a broad scope of psychosocial issues such as hookup culture, dating violence, and high risk drinking, among others, at local colleges and universities, including UCLA. In addition, Dr. Lee has served on Claremont McKenna College's Personal and Social Responsibility (PSR) Title IX and Sexual Assault Committee since its (pre-#MeToo) inception approximately five years ago. As such, she has helped draft and implement campus sexual assault prevention, education, and intervention practices. Dr. Lee also devotes considerable time and expertise to young adults on a one-on-one basis. A handpicked advisory board member of Career Up Now, Dr. Lee mentors students and recent graduates (through age twenty-six) of USC, UCLA, and California State University, Northridge (CSUN). Dr. Lee has contributed to KNBC, FOX, KTTV, and Metro News, and is a frequent consultant to the *Los Angeles Times*.

Dr. Lee received her doctorate at the University of Texas Southwestern Medical Center at Dallas—Graduate School of Biomedical Sciences, followed by a postdoctoral fellowship in behavioral medicine at Harbor-UCLA Medical Center in Torrance, California. Her independent research has been published internationally in various professional journals, including the prestigious *Journal of Affective Disorders*. She is married with two sons.

ACKNOWLEDGEMENTS

*T*o my sons David and Michael: you've certainly got to admit that we've all come a long way from that day on the beach in Laguna when you responded to my wistful dream, "You are *never* going to write a book, Mom." True at the time, because I was much more focused on my "what matters in life," which is the two of you. Thank you not only for being a positive life force that lent me the discipline and focus to write, but thank you most of all for the quiet support and bolstering of my spirits when things got rough. This book could not have been written without you guys behind me. And I am so motivated for it to be successful on behalf of you both.

Then there's my own "cherished cheerleader, avid helpmate, and trusted confidante." Thank you, John, for always believing in me, my writing, and in this book. All those shared, happy times discussing ideas with you will never be forgotten. (Even years ago, during long drives out to water polo games at CMC when I was working on initial drafts.) And thank you also for hardly ever turning down my incessant requests to read and weigh in on excerpts right down to the very end.

My publishing team at Mill City Press deserves a huge shout-out of appreciation. First, to Kate Ankofski, who never tired of my questions, and whose early assessment, suggestions, and encouragement made all the difference in making this book compelling and readable. I am also so grateful to Tricia Parker, whose gifted editorial skill proved particularly crucial not only in allowing a seamless flow of the prose, but equally if not more important for calling out any content that wasn't relevant or relatable. Thank you, Kate and Tricia.

Tremendous thanks to author coordinator Katie Tota for sharing your remarkable expertise, particularly involving "last lap" tasks in a publishing process that for me was akin to learning Russian. And immeasurable gratitude to Wallayna Bradford and Taylor McCown who took over at literally the eleventh hour, giving their all to meet a very challenging deadline.

Kudos to talented cover designer, Amanda Wright, who paid close attention to my notes and captured exactly the vibe I was looking for. And thank you in advance to my publicist, Kim Dower, for ensuring that the cover becomes well-known!

Enormous appreciation to Barbara Yancey for helping me to free up some time to devote to writing. Gratitude also to Dalita McMahon for coming to the rescue with copies whenever my printer failed (which was often). And for assisting with all those new patient calls.

I'd be remiss if I didn't acknowledge producer par excellence, Elliot Haimoff of Global Science Productions, for whom I wrote and narrated an early video of this book. Your vision and optimism proved infectious, Dr. E. Long overdue thanks additionally go to A. John Rush, MD, and Annette Brodsky, PhD, iconic pioneers in the fields of affective disorders and women's issues/ethics, respectively. I'm incredibly privileged to have been closely mentored by you both, and can only hope that the high standards you helped instill are evident in this book.

I also wish to deeply thank my endorsers, including Dr. Robert Martin, Jennifer Kaufman, Nina Sadowsky, and Sam Lewis. Your kind words and confidence made a tremendous difference to me. Thanks also to Bruce Vinokour of CAA for your early attempts to get the manuscript into the right hands. Your immensely positive reaction to what I'd written so far was exactly the "shot in the arm" I needed to continue.

Thanks to a wonderful colleague and friend, Dr. Bernard Natelson, for your support even when I was just thinking about writing a book. Flash forward to the (almost) Finish Line: your casual remarks (over Hollywood Bowl vino) regarding potential pushback from "feminists" actually compelled me to go back and elaborate in a more persuasive way — despite my own initial pushback! Bernard, thanks for having my back.

Heartfelt thanks to my Number One, Alicia Lee: you never hesitated when I ran stuff by you, and your faith in the book has been beyond helpful. But most of all, Ali, know that what I said about the best of millennial women was very much inspired by you.

Thank you to Natalie Nosek, whose enthusiasm and support for *Don't Sleep with Him Yet* has truly touched me. Plus, you get it done: I so appreciate your connecting me with author Brian Edwards, who already has been really helpful. I mostly can't wait to spend more time with you, Natalie, hopefully on an exotic island somewhere, with this book in our beach bags ...

I am forever grateful to Rabbi Laura Geller, an authentically empowered woman who has helped me dig deep into some of my own issues, a fraction of which are subtly embedded within these pages.

Special thanks to my sister Linda and to all my BFFs with whom I've laughed and cried over all sorts of our varied men/relationship experiences through the years, and who generally make life worthwhile. Ruth, particularly, you've been there from the start.

As for the first unparalleled, truly good, no, make that phenomenally *great*, man in my life, my late dad, Aaron — without both his and my mom Renee's unwavering love and support, I would be nowhere near the empowered (and badass!) woman I strive to be today.

Finally, a huge measure of gratitude is owed to my patients for sharing your stories and entrusting me with your confidences. Through the courage, openness, and honest reflection you've displayed in grappling with life's ups and downs, romance-wise and otherwise, you've already demonstrated remarkable strength in forging forward. But that's just the beginning. Although I close in on a once-faraway dream as my writing is finally done, nothing is really complete for me until these pages make a difference in you realizing your own dreams as well.